LET THERE BE LIGHT

by Roger Oakland
with Dan Wooding

"For God, who commanded the light to shine out of darkness, hath shined in our hearts, to give the light of the knowledge of the glory of God in the face of Jesus Christ" (2 Corinthians 4:6).

"Therefore if any man is in Christ, he is a new creature: old things are passed away, all things are become new" (2 Corinthians 5:17).

LET THERE BE LIGHT

by
Roger Oakland
with Dan Wooding

Table of Contents

Dedication

This book is dedicated to both the Creator and to Tyler, whose life and death the Creator used to draw me to Him and to the reality of Eternal life through Jesus Christ.

Acknowledgement

I would like to express my gratitude to my family, my wife Myrna, my sons Wade and Bryce, and my daughter Angela, for their unfailing support . . . and to thank God for all of the men He has used to mold and shape my life: Alfred Oakland, Glen McLean, Gil Killam, Lorne Pritchard, Irving Gillette, Alf Rees, John Garlock, Ed Okuhara, Chuck Smith and Romaine.

Also, I would like to thank Ron Stillman, Ed Neteland, Lela Gilbert, Jan LaRue and Barbara Westerland who all assisted in making this book possible.

Acknowledgments

Foreword

Paul speaks in Romans 1 of men who did not want to retain God in their knowledge, so they gave themselves over to their empty imaginations to try to explain the creation apart from a creator. He declared that professing themselves to be wise they actually became fools as they worshipped and served the creation rather than the Creator. These are the men, who through using their imaginations to the limit, developed the great hoax of evolution.

This book, *Let There Be Light*, shows how the deliberate deceitful teaching of the theory of evolution has had a major impact on society. And the devastating results as revealed by current events, are just what Paul warned would happen. As well, the book shows the tragic effect the humanistic lie of evolution has had on people's lives by shaping their world-view without God. But most important, it shows how God's grace and power transforms lives blinded by the lie of evolution, and how the creation message is being used today to draw many to an everlasting relationship with their Creator, Jesus Christ.

Pastor Chuck Smith
Calvary Chapel of Costa Mesa

Prologue

Throughout the centuries, countless individuals have experienced dramatic, life-changing transformations which have forever altered their courses of life. Clearly, the most incredible changes have happened to those who have had an encounter with the person of Jesus Christ.

The apostle Paul was one such individual. As he was travelling along the road to Damascus, his thoughts were consumed with ways and means of persecuting men and women, who were persistently proclaiming that Jesus was God. Suddenly and drastically, Paul's life was thrown into irreversible upheaval.

At midday, he saw a light from heaven, brighter than the sun. And as he fell to the ground with blindness, he heard a voice saying: "Saul, Saul, why are you persecuting me?"

When Saul inquired where the voice was coming from, he heard the following words:

"I am Jesus who you are persecuting. But arise and stand on your feet; for this purpose, I have appeared to you, to appoint you a minister and a witness, not only to the things which you have seen, but also to things in which I will appear to you." (Acts 26:14-16 NASB)

So it was that Saul the persecutor became Paul the evangelist.

At a later period of his life, Paul gave an account to his young friend Timothy about the amazing grace of God and how it had changed his life. He stated: "I thank Christ Jesus our Lord who has strengthened me, because he considered me faithful, putting me into service; even though I was formerly a blasphemer and a persecutor and a violent aggressor. And yet I was shown mercy, because I acted ignorantly in unbelief; and the grace of our Lord was more than abundant with the faith and love which are found in Christ Jesus." (I Timothy 1:13-14 NASB)

The book which you are about to read is written with one purpose in mind - to reflect the grace and the mercy that God made available to me, and to show how the transforming power of the gospel is relevant and active in our world today. Like Paul, I can now joyously proclaim: "I am not ashamed of the gospel, for it is the power of God for salvation." (Romans 1:16)

The gospel - the "Good News" about Jesus Christ - transformed Paul's life. It has transformed mine. My prayer is that you will allow it to do the very same for you.

Roger Oakland

Chapter One

LET'S CALL HIM TYLER

I looked at Myrna's tear-streaked face and snapped at her. "What's the matter now?" Even as I posed the curt question, I knew that I didn't really want to hear her reply.

I glanced at the table and, before she could answer, I barked impatiently, "Where's my lunch? You know I don't have time to waste. I've only got a few precious minutes before I get back to the field."

Myrna's drawn, tense face spoke volumes. I had been insensitive once again. But what was new? Our relationship had been deteriorating for a long time.

Besides, it was harvest time and nothing was important enough to interfere with the task at hand. Any farmer will tell you that there is hardly a moment to spare, even for personal problems, when you head for the harvest field at 6 A.M. and work until midnight. Myrna needed to get my food before me quickly. Then, and only then, would I listen to her problem.

Ignoring my angry response, she pressed on. "I've just come from the doctor's office in town." Her voice broke with emotion. "The X-rays have come back, and it looks as if the baby has some major developmental problems. The doctor is sending me to the city for further tests."

Her words stopped me cold, and we stared at each other blankly. Myrna had a degree in nursing and had majored in obstetrics. I'd spent nine years of my life studying and teaching biology at the University of Saskatchewan. Because of our backgrounds we both recognized all too well that this was a serious situation.

"So what's the problem?" I said, my voice slightly softer. "Tell me in biological terms what the doctor said."

Myrna took a deep breath. Her voice was barely audible. "He thinks the baby is an anacephalic."

For an instant, I was frozen. Then a sick, sinking feeling rose in my stomach. This medical term meant that the baby's brain case was not developed and that therefore, it could not survive birth. The infant could hold its own in the womb, with its heart beating and limbs moving, but as soon as it came into this world, it would die.

I managed to keep quiet, realizing how vulnerable Myrna was at this moment. One word out of place would devastate her. I was feeling rather vulnerable myself, numbly shaking my head, trying not to believe what I had just heard.

We already had two sons, Wade age 4 and Bryce age 3, but this child was to be special. This unborn infant was going to bring our collapsing marriage back together - we had planned it that way. But now hope was being snatched away from us.

I turned my head to hide my tears, then took my wife of nine years in my arms. I fumbled for something to say. "Maybe the doctor's wrong. Maybe he's been looking at the wrong X-rays. Maybe the tests were incomplete..."

Even as I spoke, my words rang hollow in my ears. This tragic loss would probably spell death for our life together. I stared at my wife without moving, without blinking.

"They've already made the arrangements for further tests at the University Hospital in Saskatoon," she murmured, her voice trailing away.

When she returned to preparing my lunch, I stared out the window. I saw our two boys playing happily outside in the August heat. Little did they know that the ground was collapsing beneath their parents.

By now it was 1977. Our marital difficulties had grown worse since I'd quit my job as a biology department assistant at the University of Saskatchewan. That job had involved both the supervision of instructors and teaching responsibilities. I had worked my way up from the bottom rung and had done all the right things to attain my position.

But before long, I had grown tired of the cynical university world. Power trips and egos seemed to dominate much of life there. True, I was a success at what I was doing, but as far as I was concerned, there was no future in continuing. It was a job, but I wanted to have money, real money. I just wanted to do what I wanted.

Sadly, during my studies and university teaching job, my marriage relationship with Myrna had begun to disintegrate. Rather than being completely devoted to my wife, I had become totally devoted to myself. I was the center of my own universe, and personal success had become my god.

What a change had taken place since I'd first entered that hallowed school of learning. My God-fearing, Bible believing parents had instilled in me a system of values based on Biblical principles. However, after nine years at the university, I had changed into a completely different person. My world view was centered around total trust in human reasoning. To me Christianity was just a "myth" for "weak-minded people." I had been converted to the philosophy of the sixties: God was dead and man would bring utopia to the earth through science and technology. My trust was in humanity, rather than in God.

In the process, I had become extremely contemptuous toward anyone who confronted me with what I perceived as a narrow-minded Christian world view. I loved to declare my humanistic opinions to anyone who would listen. To put it bluntly, I had a massive chip on my shoulder. I saw Christians as a manipulative group of emotional fanatics who had no grasp on scientific reality.

This perspective had been partly developed by an incident that had occurred when I was fourteen years old. A high-powered evangelist from eastern Canada had come to our small high school auditorium for a week-long crusade. Along with my mother and a number of other people from the community including my school friends, I went to hear this preacher.

I was transfixed by his presentation and followed his dramatic movements with astonishment. Like a caged tiger, the man prowled from side to side of the platform. With great theatrics, he described hell as "a burning torment." And as he depicted the golden streets of heaven, the congregation roared their approval with a loud "Amen!" The preacher's voice thundered through speakers that were mounted on either side of the platform. I listened in awe.

At the end of his emotionally-exhausting sermon, the evangelist asked for "all heads to be bowed and every eye closed." He asked those who wanted to go to heaven to put up their hands. Somewhat apprehensive, my hand was lifted, but barely above my shoulder.

He continued, his own hands raised in a kind of benediction, saying, "All those who raised their hands, please come forward." I opened my eyes and stared at him, a frightened expression on my face. Sheepishly, I pulled down my hand. I wasn't about to walk past my classmates in order to make a public stand.

During his second and third appeals to "come forward" I continued to sit, immobilized in my chair. I wanted to respond but refused to be humiliated. How I wished that I and this embarrassing situation were a million miles away.

Suddenly a tap on my shoulder startled me. An older lady, seated behind me, announced quite loudly, "Son, you'd best get yourself up to the front. You don't want to burn in hell, do you?" Her hoarse words hung heavily in the air. Everyone must have heard her. I was furious, and my face burned with embarrassment.

In my desperation I shot up out of my chair. Leaving my mother in her seat, I ran frantically out the back door of the auditorium. Frozen tears stung my eyes as I raced across darkened fields. For a mile and a half I continued to run. The gray sky was spitting snow, and I pulled the cold, northeast wind into my lungs in harsh, painful gasps. My legs were numb and I clenched my teeth together to keep them from chattering.

For years afterward, I looked back on this event as an

excuse to distance myself from God. "Christianity," I repeatedly stated, "is manipulative hype based on emotions, not on reality."

Although the University of Saskatchewan had been the source of my humanistic "enlightenment," my disenchantment with both the school and my activities in the biology department there had intensified. In the process I began to feel a deep desire to return to my farming roots. Farming was deeply ingrained in my personality. For me, the university was a battle of wills. Everyone I knew was struggling to get to the top of the academic ladder.

When the opportunity came for me to return to manage my father's farm, I didn't need to make a decision. Besides removing me from the university, I sensed that it would also be healthy for our family unit to work closely together. Our boys would have the same opportunity to grow up on the farm that I had enjoyed.

Grain farming is a seasonal occupation. In Saskatchewan, once harvest is complete by the end of October, six months follow in which there is nothing to do. Those winter months are long, with temperatures often dropping to 40 degrees below zero.

In an attempt to fill those cold winter nights with activity, I joined a curling team. We travelled around the Province of Saskatchewan to weekend bonspiel competitions. Teams, consisting of four players, gathered from all over the province and competed until one was victorious.

During my university days, I had curled with a team in Saskatoon, so I had gained a lot of experience. I thrived on competing against others, and the camaraderie was a great social release. It was a good excuse to get together with people and have a party. Alcohol contributed to the sense of escape my weekend sports outings provided.

Naturally, this routine had damaged my relationship with my wife. I knew it, but I couldn't seem to do anything about it. Gradually, I reached a point where I wanted to make a change. I wanted to have what my parents had in their warm, stable relationship.

Myrna and I had discussed, before our wedding, our dream of a family. We wanted to have four children, and once they had arrived, we would live happily ever after. The dream had fallen victim to my ambitions, but maybe it wasn't too late.

"Let's take our boys and spend a month in Florida and be together as a family," I suggested to Myrna one day. "We can take in Disney World and visit all the tourist attractions."

"In fact," I added thoughtfully, "let's have another child. Maybe the birth of a baby will be the turning point that will make our relationship everything we want it to be."

Myrna had smiled gently, hopefully. "Maybe so..." she replied.

During our trip to Florida, we'd discovered that Myrna was carrying that special baby who would bond us together again.

But now the doctor's horrible prognosis had shattered our hopes. Further tests confirmed the doctor's initial findings and our worst fears. To make matters even worse, we learned that Myrna would have to carry the baby to term. Labor would be induced, and at the moment of birth, the baby would die.

At night, as we lay in bed, I could feel the movements of the baby within Myrna. Anger and bitterness flooded over me. How could this be happening to us? Things were finally coming together in our relationship, and it had looked like we just might make it. Now the window of hope was being slammed shut in our faces.

When the day of the birth and death ordeal finally arrived, we hardly spoke as I drove Myrna to the city hospital. When we stopped at a drug store to buy some last minute necessities, Myrna impulsively picked up a book to read. It was called, *The Road to Bythinia,* a Biblical novel by Frank Slaughter. Later, during a hospital visit, I asked what the book was all about.

"Oh, it's based on the life of Luke from the Bible," she answered casually.

Anger welled up inside me, and I could hardly control my voice. "How could you read a book like that at a time like this?"

"It's comforting to me," she responded quietly.

Not wanting to hurt her, I said no more. I couldn't face the pain that I knew she was about to go through. Unable to stay a minute longer, I made my way back to the farm and got involved in equipment maintenance, trying to comfort myself with the thought that the nightmare would soon be over.

Time dragged by. I struggled with a trio of powerful emotions--anger, fear and anxiety. Finally I heard the phone. When I ran to the kitchen and picked up the receiver, I heard Myrna's subdued voice. "You can come and pick me up now. It's all over."

"Are you okay?"

Without answering the question she explained, "It was a boy. Let's call him Tyler. Even though his body wasn't perfect, he was beautiful. And I know he's in heaven now."

I choked back tears. Not only had we lost a son, but we

were back to square one. After all the struggling, our marital situation seemed hopeless once again. Could we ever rebuild our relationship?

I sank down on the sofa as my jaw tightened and put my head between my knees in exhaustion. Overwhelmed with grief, I began to weep. Tears surged into my eyes and rolled in torrents down my cheeks. The pain was unbearable.

My son was dead.

I was dying too.

Chapter Two

IN THE BEGINNING

Our barn. A huge yard filled with old, weathered wooden granaries. Rows of towering poplar trees. A square, two-story house standing in the middle of nowhere. Those are early images which remain imprinted upon my mind.

I grew up on a large wheat farm in the vast Canadian prairies. Canada is one the world's most sparsely populated nations, and my particular childhood experience was one few people have ever had. For me, the farm was the best place to live on earth. Canada, the world's second largest country, was my home country, and I was proud to be a Canadian. The name Canada, I discovered at school, was thought to be derived from Kanata, the Huron-Iroquis word meaning "village" or "community."

"I'm never going to leave this place as long as I live," I remember telling my mother as I sat on her knee. "I want to be a farmer here, just like Dad. Do you suppose he'll let me?"

Mother smiled knowingly and said nothing.

Our farm signified for me, as a five year old, uncomplicated contentment and happiness. I was blithely unaware that a devastating world war had ended just a few years before and that it had claimed the lives of millions of people in Europe and the Far East. The world started and ended in the acreage we cultivated in southwestern Saskatchewan.

Our farm was situated hundreds of miles from the nearest city, in a climate of extremes. The severe heat of the summers and the brutal cold of the winters provided essentials to the development of strong character. "You've got to learn to live day by day," my father would say with homespun simplicity. "Never count your bushels until you've got the crop in the bin."

Farming on the prairie involved a life style which suited a unique kind of person. The early pioneers who first made their way to the Canadian mid-west possessed many unusual qualifications. The elements were so challenging that they had to have immense stamina. And they were exceptionally strong-willed people.

At the start of the 1900's, Western Canada was open to anyone with a trailblazing spirit. Grassland was made available for small sums of money to those who wanted to risk everything, and courageous pioneers moved west, prepared to break the soil by horse and plough. My grandfather on my father's side, Henry Oakland, was just such a person. During the early twenties, while searching for his own "land of milk and honey," he decided to homestead farmland on the great Canadian plains.

His parents had emigrated from Norway to Illinois in the

1800's. Wanting an anglicized name, they changed theirs from Ageland to Oakland. Determined to follow the pioneer spirit that drove his own parents to move from Norway, my grandfather chose to investigate the promises that beckoned to him from the wide open Canadian west. After his wife died giving birth to their sixth child, Henry Oakland left his family behind for the summer months to operate a 320 acre wheat farm in Saskatchewan.

Moving there and setting up a farming operation in those days was no easy task. Long, hard days, working from sunrise to sundown, fighting the elements at every turn soon took their toll. In the summer of 1928 my grandfather suffered a stroke. At that point, my father Alfred, who was still single and thirty-two years of age, chose to move to Canada and take over where his father had left off.

My mother, Audrey DeMott, appeared in my father's life sometime during the middle thirties. Her heritage was also rooted in the pioneering spirit that had opened up the Canadian west. Her father's parents were Huguenots who, because of Roman Catholic persecution, had fled France for Holland and subsequently had moved on to the United States. Her father, Frederick DeMott, in the early 1900's, was a travelling salesman for a meat company who came to Canada seeking property. It was in Manitoba that he met my grandmother. My mother was born in the city of Saskatoon in 1911.

In the fall of 1936, my mother left her job as a one-room country school teacher and married my father. She was twenty-five and my father was forty.

Those years were commonly called the "dirty thirties" for more than one reason. The great depression, experienced around the world, was made worse in the west by drought.

Year after year, strong winds blew the rich, fertile farmland away. Thousands of families, who had committed their life savings to agriculture on the prairie, picked up stakes and left for greener pastures. My mother and father were among those who stayed.

Eleven years after they were married, on June 2, 1947, in my father's fiftieth year, I was born at the Union Hospital in Eston, Saskatchewan.

From the earliest moment I can remember, my father was the best friend and companion I ever had. He was about 5' 7", slightly overweight, and had big knurled hands and skin that was leathery from spending too much time out of doors. His personality was mellow and kind. He had a receding hairline and his hair color was a peppery-brown. Although he was more the age of a grandfather than a father, the years between us never kept us apart. Our father-son relationship remains one of the most cherished possessions of my lifetime.

Every single memory I have of my father is good. From the time I could toddle around the farmyard, Dad constantly gave me a feeling of security and well-being. One of the biggest concerns he had was his desire to teach me valuable lessons and to expose me to experiences that would equip me for my later life.

I always looked forward to the times when we could be alone, and whether he was working around the yard fixing equipment or working in our vegetable garden, I was always at his side. The farm was his life, and I knew he wanted it to be a vital part of mine, too. During the spring and summer months, my father let me sit on his knee and steer the tractor. It was during those times, that he conveyed to me the precious principles he cherished.

His deep yet simple faith in God, the Bible, and Jesus Christ, was impressed upon me from the very beginning. On several occasions I can recall how he used illustrations from the farm to help me understand life and to illustrate what it meant to have faith.

"Let it blow, let it blow!" he remarked one day, as we watched gale-force winds pile our seeded topsoil in deep drifts. "If we didn't have the wind like this, the wheat plants wouldn't send down their roots for moisture. Too much rain early in the season makes the roots grow shallow on the surface. Then, when the hot days come in July, the crop will burn up. That's just the way the Lord causes us to grow," he explained. "If you don't have a few tough times to make you put your roots down, then when the heavy slugging comes, you'll never make it!"

One September evening, just after I had started school, I was riding in the truck with my father, picking up the threshed grain from the combine in the harvest field. Looking out of the window of the truck cab, I was fascinated with the stars and the northern lights that lit up the sky.

"Hey, Dad, how many stars do you think there are out there?" I questioned him.

"I suppose God only knows," he replied, rubbing his chin. "The Bible says that God made all the stars."

Still inquisitive, I posed another question, "Where do you think the stars end, or do they just keep on going?"

"I guess that's something you can ask when you get to heaven," he smiled. "I have a hunch the heavens just go on forever and forever. They're everlasting!

"What do you mean by everlasting, Dad?" I asked. "I don't understand..."

My questions never ceased. But whatever my father told

me, I accepted without question. He lived a lifestyle that exquisitely reflected what he believed. Rarely a night would pass that I didn't see him sitting in the living room reading the Bible before he went to bed. I never knew him to drink alcoholic beverages, and he often warned me of the "traps" that existed in the world, the ones that could hurt people and lead them astray.

Sunday School attendance at our local church was a regular weekly occurrence during my childhood and adolescence. My mother taught my class for a number of those years.

There was an incident at Sunday School that I never forgot. One of our classmates, a boy by the name of Ronnie, was the kind of kid that had a real problem being accepted by the rest of the group. Because he wasn't especially bright at school and lived on the "wrong side of the tracks," there were two strikes again him. To make matters worse, a rumor had been spread around the school that whoever sat near Ronnie was doomed to get "the fleas."

On one particular Sunday, arriving a few minutes late for the class, I found myself in the situation where there was only one seat left. Sure enough, it was next to Ronnie. Rather than sitting beside him and taking the risk of getting fleas, I left the chair empty and sat on the floor. By the disapproving look my mother gave me, I knew I was in for a lot of pain later on. Reluctantly, I picked myself up and sat next to the poor kid.

On the way home, while my mother drove the family's 1957 Oldsmobile, I received a lecture which I wouldn't soon forget.

"How would you like it if someone treated you the way you treated Ronnie?" she asked me sternly. "Haven't I taught you to treat others the same way you want to be treated?"

From that Sunday on, I sat next to Ronnie every chance I got. Needless to say, I never once got "the fleas."

The summer months on the farm were always my favorite time of the year. Living creatures have fascinated me as long as I can remember so pets played a big part in my life. My dog Toby, a friendly mongrel terrier, had grown up with me from the time I was two years old. As he got older, I dreaded the time when we would be separated by death.

One day, when I came home, Toby was not at the end of the lane to greet me as usual, his tail wagging. When I opened the door of the house and saw the serious look on my mother's face, I didn't need to ask the question. Before she could open her mouth, my face puckered and the tears began to stream down my cheeks. Even though Toby had gone blind and had been dying a slow death for the last several months, I couldn't accept the fact that my parents had chosen to put him out of his misery. I loved the dog too much and the bitter experience of facing death head-on was the most traumatic situation I had ever had to cope with.

My father took me aside and talked with me. "Will I ever see Toby again?" I sobbed, shuddering and gasping. "Will Toby go to heaven?"

My father explained to me that animals were created by God for the pleasure of man. "We should be real thankful we had a dog like Toby for all these years," he said. "Everything has to die sooner or later. Even you and me."

"I know that, Dad," I said in a slow, halting whisper, struggling for breath, "But that doesn't help me right now. Why does God allow death?"

"The Bible tells us that God cares about us so much that

He planned every day of our lives from the beginning of time," he said. "It says He knows the number of hairs we have on our heads. He even knows when a sparrow falls dead to the ground. God loves and cares for all His creation, and He holds the keys to life and death. God gives everyone of us our life, and it always ends in death. It's a fact of life we all have to learn, son."

Kind as they were, Dad's words provided little comfort for the pain that I was feeling. Toby's loss stayed with me for weeks afterwards. I lovingly built a wooden cross and frame to mark where Toby was buried, wondering whether or not I would ever see him again. Every day I walked past Toby's grave, which was located in the corner of a pasture beside a nearby railroad track.

What really haunted me was the dreaded reality that, one day, I would have to face these same feelings all over again when my father and mother died. Too horrible to contemplate, I banished those unwelcome thoughts from my mind.

Chapter Three

THE DEATH OF A CONSCIENCE

I can still recall the morning my parents and I bounced down the gravel road toward the city, before the sun had started to peek over the eastern horizon. The time for registration for university classes had come. My dad proudly sat behind the steering wheel of his freshly-polished 1963 purple Oldsmobile Delta 88. I couldn't help but smile as I looked at the clothes he was wearing. Most days he was comfortable in overalls and an old sweater, but that day he was attired in his best brown suit and a cream tie. His black shoes shone.

All through my childhood I could not once remember my parents leaving the farm during the busy summer season. For them to venture forth during harvest, even for a day, was completely unbelievable. This was clearly a very significant event in all of our lives.

For the past several years, I had worked diligently towards this goal. I had graduated from high school with an open scholarship for university. Now, however, I had mixed feelings tugging at me from all directions, and I wasn't quite sure how to deal with them. Leaving the farm. Starting a new life. Saying goodbye to my parents. Meeting new friends. Exploring new subjects. No matter what lay ahead, leaving the farm behind, especially at harvest time, had not been an easy decision for me. Still, a university education was too much of an opportunity to pass up.

As a child, one of my hobbies had been the assembling of a collection of moths and butterflies native to southwestern Saskatchewan. It was fascinating to gather caterpillars during the early summer, place them in glass jar containers, then watch their incredible transition into beautiful winged creatures. As we drove toward the university, the question continued to flash through my mind: was my life about to go through a similar metamorphosis?

Three hours after leaving home, we pulled into the outskirts of Saskatoon. This city of 177,000 is the largest in Saskatchewan and is located on the South Saskatchewan River in the south central part of the province. The first thing on the agenda was to look for a place to stay. Both my mother and father thought it would be good if I could room and board with an older retired couple who had been recommended by some friends.

Mr. and Mrs. Cochrane were a dream come true. Both my parents and I knew, the moment we entered the door of their house, that this was the place for me. I had always felt attracted to older people since a small boy. My maternal grandmother was especially close to me. I had spent hours listening to her sound words of advice as I was growing up, and she made me feel important and loved whenever she was around. The cozy atmosphere at Cochrane's gave me the same feeling of belonging.

Once my housing situation was settled, the next undertaking was to find out what classes I needed before registration took place in the afternoon. My high school science teacher had suggested that I try and get some instructions from the university biology department. Based on his counsel, we made our way to the university grounds. The impressive, 2,400 acre University of Saskatchewan campus, with its many gothic-style greystone buildings, overlooks the South Saskatchewan River.

We must have looked slightly out of place as my father drove the car through the campus at an almost funeral pace, finally parking in a visitor parking zone. A security guard noticed our confusion as we wandered aimlessly around. He came to our aid, and, at our request, he directed us to the Biology Building.

It was a great relief when a man dressed in a long white lab coat stopped us in the hall and asked what we were looking for. My father explained that I had come to the university to study biology and that we were trying to find out what classes I was required to take. The man, who obviously understood our predicament, led us to the general office. From there we were advised to meet with a professor who was in charge of counseling first-year students who were interested in majoring in biology.

"Dr. Remple, Professor of Entomology," the sign read above the second floor office. I could hardly believe my eyes. Entomology, the study of insects, was the very area of biology that interested me most. I could scarcely hide the joy that was leaping inside me.

Professor Remple was an elderly gentleman with thick, wavy, white hair. I was deeply impressed by his presence.

"What can I do for you folks, today?" he asked, seeing us standing at the open door. My eyes nearly popped out of my head when I saw the incredible butterfly collection that was displayed on his desk.

"This is the most fantastic collection I have ever seen!" I blurted out, my eyes bright with excitement. "How many years did it take for you to collect all of those?"

Modestly, he directed our attention to an entire wall of drawers. "The drawer you see here," he explained, "belongs to the large collection over there." One by one, he opened them up, allowing us to view his collection. I was finding it hard to breathe so great was my excitement. Finally, my father interrupted.

"The secretary in the general office downstairs suggested that you could help my son choose the classes he needs for his first year of university. It sure looks like we were sent to the right place."

"Well that's great," Dr. Remple said as he enthusiastically gripped my hand. "Let's see what I can come up with." While he was talking, my mother was busy digging through her purse, trying to locate my final grades from high school.

"Our son really enjoys biology," she said. "That's where he got his highest grades." The professor scanned my report card, then looked me straight in the face. "Your high school marks are certainly very good." he said. "But allow me to offer you some words of advice. Classes at university will be very different from anything you've had before. Be prepared to see your grade point average drop substantially. Still, as long as you work hard, and listen to what your professors tell you, I know you can do well."

Dr. Remple pulled a university directory from his bookshelf and began to flip through the pages. "If you have an interest in biology as your major," he explained, "You'll require these subjects for your first year: biology, chemistry, English, math and philosophy."

"Philosophy?" I blurted out. I had never even heard the word before. "Why do I have to take philosophy?"

"That's one of the required courses you are expected to take here at university," Dr. Remple replied. "A university education based totally on the natural sciences would give you a very narrow view of the world. Classes like philosophy, English and sociology will open your mind to new areas that will broaden your experience. They may not appeal to you now, but you'll understand their significance later on."

The classes that were suggested for me were certainly not the ones I would have picked out. I had envisioned majoring in biology. And, to me, majoring in something meant studying nothing else. Somewhat disappointed, we thanked the professor for his help and made our way to the registration line.

Finally, with all our tasks completed, the end of the day arrived. I was dropped off at my boarding house, barely able to fight off the troubled feelings that were already stirring inside me. I watched my parents' car pull away and choked back tears. As I lay on my bed, I put my hands behind my head and stared vacantly up at the ceiling.

"How fortunate I am to have parents like mine," I thought. "I'll do everything in my power to make them proud of me."

The first few weeks of classes, compared to what I had been used to in high school, were like suddenly finding myself in a foreign land without being able to speak the language. Instead of being acquainted with every one of my classmates, I knew no one. In fact, I was just one of ten thousand anonymous students, wandering around from building to building, class to class. Instead of thirty students in a classroom, there were two to three hundred. I had never seen so many people in all my life. In fact, there were on campus a large number of foreign students representing nearly every country and religion of the world.

One of the biggest difficulties that confronted me was the adjustment I was having to make in my own thinking. The philosophy professor was the first major obstacle I faced. His whole line of teaching was confusing to me. He taught that moral standards and ethical views were situational and relative. He said that reality was make-believe because "belief is what you make it." The idea that a person could create his or her reality seemed foolish. In fact, within the period of just a few classes, he challenged everything I had been brought up to believe and accept as a child.

The English course was even more confusing. English, I thought, was the study of how to properly use the language. Instead, the course was centered around some author's opinion of what he or she figured life was all about.

Sad to say, biology was the biggest stumbling block of all. For the first two weeks, the topic of every lecture was centered around the subject of the origin of life. The word "evolution," which had never been in my vocabulary before, was repeated over and over again.

"Darwinian Evolution" seemed to be an absolute obsession with the professor, and he endeavored to make the class believe every single word he was saying.

One particular lecture annoyed me. "Scientists are not certain how it happened," the professor said, "but they believe that non-life became life billions of years ago in the shallow waters of an unknown sea." He continued to expound this theory in more detail.

"Lightning striking the earth's atmosphere made up of primitive gasses, created the first building blocks of life. The building blocks rained out of the atmosphere into the oceans and made a kind of 'chicken soup' in which random collisions occurred. Eventually, the first self-replicating molecule was formed by accident, and, as soon as a molecule appeared that could divide and reproduce itself, a major law was broken for the first time and the formation of life was well on the way."

Science, I had been taught in high school, was based on observable, testable evidence. This new theory seemed to me to be speculative and unreasonable. And although I had not embraced Christianity, I still believed there had to be a God.

The first set of university exams came sooner than I had expected. However, I had prepared myself through many hours of study. The biology exam was easy, I thought. In spite of the problem I had with the subject material early in the term, the rest of it was becoming new and exciting. I walked out of the exam with a feeling of satisfaction and accomplishment. A week later, when the marks were posted, I was shocked beyond belief. My name was no where to be seen.

Certain that my examination paper had been lost, I made an appointment to see my professor, the head of the Biology Department. With a sweep of his hand, he motioned me to sit on a chair in front of his desk. He flipped through a huge stack of papers until he came to mine. A stern look hardened his face as he scrutinized my paper. He paused for a moment. "You are wasting your time and your parents' money," he finally said, glaring menacingly at me over the top of the glasses that were perched on the end of his nose.

"What's wrong?" I could scarcely whisper the question. As my eyes scanned the front page, I could see angry lines from a red marking pen scribbled across the entire page. There was no question about it, the handwriting was my own. It was my exam. But what had I written that had made this man so violently upset?

"Do you recall the first question on this exam?" Before I had a chance to open my mouth he continued. "I did not ask you to answer the question with your opinion. I asked for the answer to, 'How did life originate?'" His voice was sarcastic, and his mouth was hard.

At that moment, I knew exactly what had happened. Instead of answering his question the way he had taught us in class, I had given my own view of creation as I had always accepted it. I needed no further explanation.

"I'm very sorry, sir," I responded meekly, "but what about the rest of the questions that I answered. What did I do wrong there?" He rapidly flipped through each page, deliberately keeping the paper out of my sight.

"The next exam, you'll do better if you listen to what I tell you now!" He took a deep breath and let it out slowly. "University exams are designed to find out what you have learned in class. Answer the questions the way you've been taught in class and you'll do fine." With that, he finally smiled, although rather insincerely.

I had never before failed an exam, and his words echoed over and over again through my head. In a dazed trance, I picked myself up out of the chair and left his office. Never in my life had I felt so deflated. I had answered the questions on origins the only way my conscience would allow me to, and I had failed the entire exam.

"I'm sure he didn't even correct the rest of the paper," I muttered under my breath.

Full of despair, I stumbled out of the office in a daze and walked to the "Bowl," a large, oval piece of grassland, fringed by greystone varsity buildings and filled with huge trees that were beginning to shed their rust-colored leaves. Still stunned, I sat down on the grass and tried to eat my lunch. I had no appetite; I felt depressed and wanted to quit and go home. The thought of being on the farm was infinitely more attractive than the frustration I was experiencing at the moment.

And yet, conflicting thoughts began to flash through my mind. I had promised my parents I would be a success. If I quit now, I would be a failure and a disgrace to them.

"What's the matter with you, Oakland? Has your best friend dropped dead?" I heard a familiar voice ask, interrupting my unhappy thoughts. I saw Ross, my biology lab partner, standing directly in front of me. Beside him stood a girl he introduced as his sister, a third-year student.

"You look like the world is about to come to an end!" He didn't seem to know when to quit.

"That's exactly how I feel right now," I said, still trembling. "What's put you into such a good mood?"

"I passed the biology exam we had last week," he gloated. "Not bad, considering over half the class never made it."

"That's just the reason I'm so down in the dumps right now," I said. "I've just come back from the professor's office. I went there to find out why my name hadn't been posted. Now I wish I hadn't bothered".

"What mark did you get?" Ross was determined to get to the bottom of the problem. Reluctantly, I told him what had occurred when I had gone to see the professor.

"Well, that doesn't surprise me one bit," Ross said. "But forget about what happened, Roger, and get on with the course. The first set of mid-terms don't count for anything towards the final mark at the end of the year. Just toss away your foolish religious ideas and get on with bigger and better things."

"That might be easy for you", I responded defensively. "But it sure isn't for me. What we were told about evolution not only doesn't make any sense to me, but it's not true. In fact, it's pure nonsense! I just couldn't accept what he was telling me. It contradicts everything I have ever believed. My conscience won't allow me to do it!"

"You might as well go back to the farm then," Ross interjected. "Those kind of narrow-minded religious views disappeared from intellectual circles eons ago. You're still living in the dark ages. Listen, my friend. Let me give you a piece of valuable advice. If you are going to get anywhere at all in this world, you're going to have to keep up with the times. Creation is just a myth that somebody wrote about in a book. It was dreamed up by a bunch of uneducated old men thousands of years ago!"

He paused, then added, "You'll have to learn to flow with the river or you'll drown."

Ross' sister, who had overheard the conversation, chipped in with her comments. "Sounds to me like you're in the wrong major," she said, a slight edge in her voice. "Maybe you should go in for theology. If you are going to take biology, you'll have to get used to the fact that the entire subject is based on evolution. Evolution isn't a theory; it's a fact! Everyone in the scientific community accepts that without question. If you are going to get anywhere at all, you'll have to make up your mind to discard your childish views and become open-minded."

Over the next few days, I spent a lot of time pondering what Ross and his sister had told me during our conversation. When I had made a choice to come to university, I had no idea that the subject I liked most would end up challenging what I believed about God being the Creator of life. Yet, I could clearly see what Ross and his sister had said was accurate. I had to make a choice. My confrontation with the biology professor had convinced me that there was no room to express any viewpoint other than his - and the school's.

I wondered what my mother and father would think if they knew what the courses at the University of Saskatchewan were teaching me. Maybe it didn't really matter, I began to rationalize. They would never even have to know what my classes were all about. In fact, how could I explain it to them in words they would understand? Besides, if making a decision to accept the evolutionary view meant a choice between failure and success, then the decision had already been made.

I had to be a success, and therefore I would pay the Biology Department lip service.

From that point of view, my studies went smoothly. As time passed, some of the ideas I had rejected when I first began university actually became challenging and informative. Biology continued to fascinate me far above all the other classes; I admired the years of study and research that had unveiled the amazing complexity of living things. What an amazing amount of knowledge had been accumulated through the efforts of renowned men and women of science. I dreamed that one day I, too, would become a contributor.

Christmas exams went well. This time, when the marks were posted, my name was at the top of the list. Only six students out of the class of 250 had received an "A" grade, and I was one of them.

My emotions were bursting at the seams. From the brink of absolute failure only a few months earlier, now I was sitting on top of the world. There was no question about it. The right decision had been made.

One day, as I opened my mail, my heart leapt at the sight of a personal letter from the head of the Biology Department. He was inviting me to a special party for all the students who had earned an "A" on their Christmas exam. There were only six of us invited and I had beaten all the odds. It was high praise.

Later on, as I rubbed shoulders with the professors in the faculty lounge, I was overwhelmed by a feeling of suppressed excitement. I had made a firm decision. I would do anything to succeed in university.

I would do it, even if it meant the death of a conscience - my conscience. And now I was old enough to make my own decision. My choice was clear.

Chapter Four

SUMMER OF CHANGE

"**O**ne or two drinks won't hurt you! What's the matter with you, Oakland? Don't be such a party pooper. Join the good life and have some fun!" I was on a ski trip to the Canadian Rockies following my final first-year exams. This celebration at the end of the year was offering me my first opportunity to experiment with alcohol.

As a youth, I had often assessed the "pros and cons" of alcohol consumption. My parents' lifestyle simply did not permit the presence of this mind-altering product in our home. On a number of occasions, my father had pointed out to me the short-term and long-term effects of the habit.

There had never been a doubt in my mind all through my adolescent years that my parents were right in their position. They had convinced me that the positive effects associated with the use of alcohol simply did not exist. Even during my entire first year away from home, when a number of opportunities were presented to have a drink or two, the decision for me to say "no" wasn't a problem.

But, at the moment, I was caught in a dilemma that I had never experienced before. There was no doubt about it. My first year had brought about a real change in the way I viewed myself and others. The very idea that the world operated so much differently than I had been brought up to believe was beginning to alter my lifestyle. Many times throughout the year I had been challenged to reconsider my own childish perception of life.

"Perhaps I am wrong," I said to myself. Maybe I've missed some great adventures by hanging onto prohibitive moral standards. Who can really say what's right and what's wrong? After all, look how naive I was about the origin of life. If I hadn't been exposed to evolutionary teaching, I would have gone through life robbed of the truth about origins.

There was no question about it, my generation belonged to a new era of enlightenment. Perhaps what I had learned in less than a year away from home was the beginning of a new and exciting era of my own personal existence.

"Sure, why not?" I replied, almost embarrassed that I had first refused the offer. Yet there was a silent voice from deep within me that momentarily caused me to pull my hand away. I could hear my father's words echoing in my mind: "If you never take the first drink, then you'll never have to make a decision later in life to take the last."

By then it was too late to change my decision. I took the drink. It didn't seem like a dramatic event at the time. In fact, life went right on for months, even years, afterwards as if nothing had happened. My grades remained good. My intellectual successes were rewarding. I was a respected man on campus.

One of the greatest reasons for the academic success that I had achieved through my first year was a girl named Myrna Underschute. A beautiful blonde teenager, she had first captured my attention at a summertime drive-in movie.

I was captivated by her lively blue eyes, sparkling with light.

"Now don't forget to write," she had instructed me as we parted to go our separate ways. I couldn't help but notice that her face was flushed with color. Soon letters were spanning the miles between us, and this lovely young woman was consuming all my waking thoughts.

From the very beginning, Myrna and I both knew that the love we shared would lead to a lifetime partnership. A few years later, our relationship was crowned by the wonderful moment when I officially asked her to be my bride and slipped an engagement ring on her left hand.

Whenever I wasn't busy with my studies, my spare time was spent with Myrna and her family. She always seemed to provide me with the encouragement I needed. Her support helped me to keep going.

My goals and dreams became her goals and dreams also. Through my first two years of classes at the university, Myrna was completing her last two years at high school. We had planned that when she graduated from school she would enter the College of Nursing on the same campus where I was attending. Following the completion of her first year we would get married. By then we would have known each other five years.

The big day was to be the twenty-second day of June, 1968. And it was not only the debilitating heat that caused beads of perspiration to break out on my face as I waited in the campus United Church of Canada chapel.

"Where is she?" I almost shouted to my best man, Ken Ryde, my former roommate.

We had picked the gray, hand-quarried limestone chapel for no other reason than that it was on campus where both of us had attended university.

The seconds ticked by like hours and I began to wonder if Myrna had cold feet and decided not to go ahead with our plans. "What a humiliation it will be if she doesn't come now," I thought to myself. All of our friends and relatives were there to witness the event. Suppose she was a "no show?"

I checked my watch again. It was now five minutes past three o'clock, five minutes after we were due to start the ceremony.

"She's here," Ken exclaimed as he saw Myrna, dressed in a gorgeous white dress, a veil covering her pretty face. She arrived at the entrance of the chapel on her father's arm.

Taking a deep breath, I was soon gazing down the aisle, watching Myrna gracefully walking toward me. She looked like a fairy princess. I was fully convinced, at that moment, that our life together would be nothing short of wonderful. We had so carefully planned this event, and had prepared for it for such a long time. What could possibly go wrong now?

My peripheral vision caught sight of my mother and father, sitting proudly on the front row along with Grandmother Allan who, despite the suffocating heat, was wearing a large fox fur around her shoulders.

It seemed like a blur as the minister went through the wedding vows with us: "For better, for worse, for richer, for poorer, in sickness and in health, till death do you part."

He beamed as I put on the gold band on Myrna's left hand and said, a twinkle in his eye, "Roger, you may now kiss the bride."

We both knew, as we exchanged that first kiss as man and wife, that we were entering a new doorway into happiness. I had graduated with distinction, and now I was married! My father had promised me a share of the farm and had provided a place for us to begin our new married life together. I knew, beyond a shadow of a doubt, that Myrna and I would live happily ever afterwards.

Following our honeymoon on beautiful Vancouver Island in British Columbia, we planned to spend the summer helping my father on the farm until the fall term at the university began.

During that summer, the long hours of riding the tractor around the fields provided me with plenty of time to further evaluate my life and the direction in which I was heading. My years at the university had continued to change my point of view. One night at the supper, Myrna noticed that I was lost in thought.

"Don't you like the food?" she queried, a puzzled look crossing her face.

"No, that's not the problem," I sighed. "I have been thinking all day about the future. The older generation doesn't seem to have a clue what is happening. They are so locked up in the past that they don't understand where we are or where our generation is headed."

Myrna shook her head mutely. She was unsure whether to probe my thoughts with questions or keep her curiosity to herself.

By now a tremendous gap had widened between my new-found beliefs and lifestyle and those I had held in my youth. I longed for a chance to share with my parents the new dimension of understanding I had gained. At the same time, I knew that any such conversation would prove useless. In fact, it was almost frightening for me to imagine where I would even begin.

One evening, just a week or so before the fall semester, the opportunity presented itself for the long-anticipated conversation. I had stopped by my parents' house to talk with my father, to find out what work he was planning for us to do on the following day. He was seated in his favorite living room chair with his transistor radio perched on his lap.

As long as I could remember, my father had tuned in "The Haven of Rest," a daily Christian broadcast from Hollywood, California. That day was no exception. As a child, I had often sat beside him and listened to the program. The same music, the same voice and the same message still blared over the radio's speaker.

"Why did I have to come here now?" I grumbled wearily to myself. "This is the very thing that gets under my skin. Why doesn't he listen to something else for a change?

"Sit down, Roger, and listen with me. We'll talk later," my father motioned toward a nearby chair.

"Why do you insist on listening to that same message over and over again," I began, my voice rising with ill-concealed annoyance. "I can't be bothered wasting my time. I'll wait in the other room till its over." I rebelliously stomped out and plopped down at the kitchen table.

My father never lost his temper with me. And that day was no exception. But he wasn't about to let the incident pass without a word.

He shut off the radio, followed me into the kitchen and sat

down at the opposite end of the large kitchen table.

"Perhaps we should have a talk," he began slowly. "In fact, I've wanted to sit down and discuss some things with you for quite a while."

"All right, let's talk, Dad," I declared boldly. "What's on your mind?"

"Why don't you want to listen to my favorite radio program?" he began. "What's happened to you lately? It seems that the eagerness you once had as a small boy to go to church has been replaced with a whole different attitude. The only time you've been inside the door of the church over the past few years was the day you were married."

"Seeing as you've asked me, I'll tell you, Dad," I responded haughtily. "Maybe you get some sort of comfort and enjoyment out of listening to that Bible talk over and over again, but for me, it's pure nonsense,"

So began my diatribe. "How can you structure your life around a book that was written thousands of years ago and has no application for the world we live in today? Let's face it, the Bible is obsolete. It's a collection of myths."

In a way, I felt guilty attacking my father's long-held beliefs. But I wasn't able to hold myself back now that the conversation was underway. Besides, my father was determined to hear more of what I had to say.

"What part of the Bible are you having a problem with?" he asked gently, his voice still even.

"The whole thing!" I snapped back. "But if you want to begin somewhere, the first verse of the first chapter would be a good place to start."

It was like a cork had been pulled from a bottle and words were tumbling out all over one another, helter skelter. "For example, the idea of creation as described in the book of

Genesis is nothing more than a Babylonian myth. The story has no scientific merit at all. And if you can't accept the very first chapter of the Bible, how is it possible to trust any of the rest of it, either?"

By this time, my mother, who had been washing the dishes, moved over to the table and sat down next to me. She had overheard everything and couldn't keep quiet any longer.

"You certainly don't sound like the boy we used to know," she stared at me with stricken eyes. "Whatever has happened that would make you change your mind the way you have? I had to look twice to see if it was really you saying those things."

"Mother," I blurted out emotionally, "It has a lot to do with common sense and education. Scientists have proven beyond a shadow of a doubt that all life is the product of evolution and change which has gradually taken place over billions of years of the earth's history.

"The whole idea of a Creator and a special creation was put forward by a primitive people of the past who didn't have an understanding of the mechanisms found in nature. Now that scientists have studied the evidence from biology and geology and can trace the development of life from the past to the present, there is no need for the myth of creation."

To me, knowledge was power. And I, as a university student now, had lots of knowledge.

Dad patiently allowed me to finish my argument and then re-entered the discussion. "I'm not sure I know what you mean by evolution and development of life," he said.

"Evolution," I explained, giving my father a condescending glance, "is an explanation of the origin of life without the supernatural. It's based on natural laws that scientists can observe. Mankind holds no special place in the universe. For the present, we just represent the level of intelligence that has resulted from billions of years of random chance events."

"Where on earth did you ever come up with this?" my mother exclaimed, a hint of sadness in her voice. "Your ideas make no sense at all to me."

"I'll try to explain it further, then," I replied, arrogant in my scholarly superiority. The discussion had gone too far to let it drop where it was.

"The traditional views that our society has accepted in the past are changing. We are entering one of the greatest periods of history this earth has ever known. The human race has evolved to a level where it can now direct the future of planet earth. Through tremendous advancements by man, we have come to a time where we can make the world a better place to live--not only for humankind, but for the ancestral forms of life from which we have evolved."

"But where do you find room for God in this kind of thinking?" my mother challenged. "How do you explain the presence of life on this earth without a Creator?"

"Mother, it's hard for me to explain this to you, since you've never gone to university," I said. "When we are honest with the facts, there is insufficient evidence for the belief in the existence of the supernatural realm. If we rely on outdated Judeo-Christian views as we have in the past, the question of human survival is in jeopardy.

"As a student of science, I am instructed to begin with the visible, not the invisible. Natural science is the reality that is before us, not some deity which is only a figment of the imagination of man."

Both my mother and father stared at me in amazement. I decided to add to their astonishment. "Nature may indeed be much more complex than we think," I stated, launching into my version of a filibuster. "In fact, just about every day, science uncovers more and more knowledge. But the fact remains that we can find no special purpose or providence for the human species. Humans are totally responsible for what we are and what we will become. No deity will ever save us. We must take the responsibility to save ourselves."

Dad couldn't restrain himself. "And how do you think that will happen?" His usually good-humored face looked weary and sober.

"Just think back through your lifetime and add up the changes you have seen," I quickly responded. "Would you have ever believed the things that have taken place in the area of medicine and technology alone? Just think, in your life-span, which is just a shadow compared to the history of life, man has gone from the horse-and-buggy-era, all the way to placing a man on the moon. If we can do that, then what lies ahead when we start to use the human brain to its fullest potential?"

"What do you mean by that?"

"Scientists estimate that most human beings only tap into ten-percent or less of their brain's capacity. There are all kinds of people in the world today who are determined to expand that potential for the benefit of mankind. And I believe it will happen!"

My father had heard enough. "Roger," he said in a reproving voice, "your whole view dumbfounds me. I don't have the education you do, but if the kind of thinking you are reflecting is the product of education, I am sorry to say that I believe you are sadly mistaken.

"Whether you agree with it or not, the Bible teaches that man's ideas compared with God's are mere foolishness. You may not agree with me now, but some day you will find out what I am saying is Truth."

Impatiently, I interrupted. "That seems to be the reason we are having this discussion, Dad. Your understanding of truth is based on the Bible. At one time in my life, I believed the same way as you. I suppose if I hadn't had the opportunity to be exposed to some other views, I would still be locked into that same narrow framework."

Mercifully, the discussion came to an end. I left feeling sorry for my parents. I had overpowered them with my superior intelligence, but they were just too set in their ways to change. I shook my head in frustration as I walked away.

Was there no way I could make them understand my advanced, intellectually brilliant arguments?

Chapter Five

THE DEDICATED INSTRUCTOR

All through school there was one thing I knew for sure - a teaching position was the last job in the world I would ever consider. A person would have to be insane to suffer that kind of abuse. That's what I'd always told myself. But somehow time and circumstances have a way of reshaping former ideas. After completing my degree in Biology, I was asked if I would consider an instructor's position at the Biology Department, teaching first and second year Biology students. The job would provide me with full-time employment throughout the winter term.

"It looks like I'll have to eat my words and change my mind about the teaching profession," I found myself telling Myrna one day.

Despite my preconceived notions, the offer was appealing to me. My share of the living provided by the family grain farm was not sufficient to allow me the luxury of relaxing during the winter months. And Myrna was still working toward her degree in nursing. Both of us attending classes at the same time was expensive - too expensive to handle without my taking a job.

Besides the money, there were also several side benefits that made the job seem even more attractive. Not only would I be involved in teaching and in the preparation of class material, but it would also be possible for me to continue taking classes in order to advance my own education in the area of the biological sciences. That was, as far as I was concerned, the best of both worlds.

As it turned out, teaching was far more exciting than I'd ever thought possible. Not only was it rewarding, but it also allowed me to be involved in explaining the mysterious processes of life to others. Toward the end of the first year, I was advised by the head of the Biology Department that my supervisor was resigning and I had been recommended for her position. It all seemed too good to be true. I was on my way upward, moving rapidly toward academic success.

The following year, I started out the term as supervisor of the lab instructors. My major responsibility was to organize the lab portion of the introductory biology classes. Every week, new lab material was introduced to the students, and it was my job to make sure the classes ran smoothly.

The first-year class consisted of 900 students, divided into lab sections of fifty. I was supposed make sure things went according to plan and that the instructors were properly prepared to teach the classes and answer questions relating to the subject material. There were usually twenty to thirty instructors to brief each week. Most of these instructors were graduate students who used the part-time work to help with their financial support.

When examination time rolled around, I also created the examinations and corrected them. The lab portion of the biology classes counted for fifty percent of the student's final mark, so it was a major concern of mine to see that the students were taught correctly.

One of the primary observations I made, as a supervisor, was that most students could go through an entire year of introductory biology classes and still not have a real grasp of the basics. Students were overwhelmed by the volume of detailed information they were receiving. With so much to absorb, it was quite possible for them to miss the unifying theme of the course.

Central to the study of biology were two areas that concerned me the most - cell division and the pivotal importance of evolution. The correcting of thousands of examination papers each year, along with holding discussions with numerous students, confirmed my suspicions. Most of them simply did not give evolution the credit it was due. That was something I was determined to change.

On occasion, I would stop a student on campus and ask him questions as a sort of informal survey of his general understanding of the course. This further convinced me that the significance of evolution needed to be stressed much more clearly. A number of students were quite vocal in their position that "it was only fair" to teach the creation explanation alongside what they considered the "theory" of evolution.

There was a growing concern throughout the Biology Department that the teaching of science in the public schools needed to be upgraded with evolutionary teaching. "If there is only one thing that our students remember when they leave this institution," I would remind the lab instructors, "it must be the unifying theme of evolution."

A number of the biology faculty members were also concerned that evolution be stressed to a far greater degree. Several of the professors were deeply upset over the fact that high school students were not being properly grounded. I was personally able to convey to the teaching staff the awakening I had received to the reality of evolution during my first year of university classes.

"It is important that we do something about this problem, and that it be done soon," one of the senior professors stated at a staff meeting. "If we do not address this issue, the integrity and effectiveness of our educational system is at risk. To remain silent would be a disgrace. It would compromise the very fundamental principles of scientific thought." I enthusiastically nodded in agreement.

The consensus of the teaching staff was that we should encourage the Provincial Department of Education to make some necessary changes to the existing high school biology course. We were also aware that the religious views that students might attempt to put forward in a classroom situation had to be suppressed.

There were always a number of students each year who vocally expressed their concern over the teaching of the evolutionary view. I personally made a point of finding out who the dissidents were and addressing the issue with them.

One such troublemaker was a young man named Ed. By the end of the first term of classes, Ed's truculent reputation was well-known throughout the department. At coffee breaks, the professor who taught the theory portion of the biology class that Ed was taking, often conveyed to the rest of the faculty how exasperated he was with Ed's questions.

"Most students just simply accept what is taught in class," the professor related. "This guy questions absolutely every word I say. He has been so brainwashed by religion, he can't even begin to think for himself."

Some of the instructors had also been complaining to me about Ed. Certainly, I vowed, this kind of disruption could not take place unchecked any longer. The next week, when Ed's lab was in process, I made a special point of finding out where he was seated. Surveying the class, I stopped at Ed's desk and asked him how he was enjoying the course. He immediately started to tell me what he thought about the emphasis on evolution. So that a disturbance would not occur in front of the rest of the class, I invited Ed to my office after the lab to talk over his concern.

Later that same day, Ed appeared at my office. I was surprised that he had taken up my offer so soon. He opened the door without knocking and stood before my desk. I observed my quarry for a moment and then indicated that he should sit down.

"What seems to be the problem?" I asked, as he sank into the chair. I wanted to crush this rebellion under my heel, quickly and completely. "I understand you are concerned that this class is not being taught with your interests in mind. Is that correct?"

I tapped my finger on my desk to communicate my frustration.

He was quick to answer. "Well, sir, that is not exactly right," he responded, a wry smile curving his mouth. "The problem I am having with university biology is that it appears to based upon the assumption that evolution is a fact.

Before I came to this institution, I had always been taught that evolution was just a theory."

"I suppose you are right in that view," I said, keeping my voice on an even tone, but already feeling uncomfortable. "But let me try and clarify for you why evolution is accepted as fact and not just as theory."

"First of all," I said, rising to my feet, hoping this would intimidate him, "I must remind you how science works. Scientists operate within a system designed for continuous testing. Scientists are always open to corrections and new findings by other scientists. Until an idea has been sufficiently tested, it is called a hypothesis. When a hypothesis has survived repeated opportunities for disproof, it then becomes an accepted theory. A theory that has withstood as many severe tests as, for example, that of biological evolution is held to with a very high degree of confidence."

Ed could hardly sit still as he listened to me making my point. "That's the whole reason I strongly disagree with what is being taught here," he blurted out in a faintly belligerent tone, his cheeks flushing. "The whole idea that life could develop from non-life is totally absurd! There is no testable scientific proof for that at all."

"Then what other explanation do you have for the origin of life?" I asked pointedly. My question was deliberately designed to get Ed to bring up the Bible.

"Every intelligent being has two choices," Ed replied, after thinking for a moment. "At least, that's the way I look at it. Either life came on the scene as the result of a Creator, or it happened because of random chance. My common sense leads me to believe in the concept of a Creator."

Not getting the answer that I had wanted, I attempted to

put words in Ed's mouth. "I would suspect your view is highly influenced by your belief in the Bible. Am I right?"

"I guess you're right," he replied. I could almost see the computer clicking in his mind behind his eyes. "But until someone can show me a more sensible explanation of how life originated, then I am more than satisfied with the Biblical view."

"Well, unfortunately for you Ed, the Bible is not a required text for this course," I said, smiling benevolently. "There is absolutely no room for the Biblical perspective in a science classroom. You see, the Science of Biology seeks to understand the living world we see around us by observation and experimentation. One of the characteristics of a person who researches in the area of science is an open-minded personality. When you rely on the Bible for 'revelation' then you are no longer open-minded. The conclusion which you have drawn from your creationist point of view cannot be tested and therefore can have no place in a scientific discussion."

"Let's leave the Bible out of this discussion for the moment," Ed interjected, holding my eyes with a steady gaze, "and evaluate your statement that science is based on observation and experimentation. If that is the case, how can you tell me that evolution is scientific? How can you maintain that non-life has evolved into complex life when no one has ever observed this happening? Every form of life we see in the world around us today has arisen from life which already exists. If evolution is a fact, then show me the facts that prove non-life can become life."

"The theory of evolution does not teach that life is evolving from non-life today," I responded, enjoying the verbal jousting. "If that is your view of evolution, then you have not understood what you have been taught in class. Primitive, simple, single-celled life evolved from non-life millions of years ago in the past when conditions on the earth were very much different from what they are today.

"Scientists believe the development of order from non-living material to living cells occurred totally based upon the laws of probability and chance," I continued, my eyes fastening on his. "The basic building blocks of life, including the amino acids and nucleotides, were made when lightning bolts flashed through the earth's primitive atmosphere. Given enough of these building blocks, it was then only a matter of time that the first self-replicating cell came into being. As soon as the waters were populated with the first cells, the conditions were then available for Darwin's theory of natural selection to take place."

"What do you mean by natural selection?" Ed interrupted.

"I mean that the pressures of the environment began to discriminate or select between the different types of cells that had come into existence." By now I was hardly pausing for breath. I was surprised to see that Ed was actually listening to what I had to say. So I pressed on. "The environment acts as a mechanism which picks out the cells which are most suitable, pruning out the stock of those that do not perform as well. As this process continues, over eons of time, life improves. Life then proceeds in the direction from simple to complex and up the ladder to eventually become man. Every credible biologist accepts this. The evidence is indisputable."

Ed was incredulous. "It's nothing but a story!" he scoffed. "A fairy tale, though, would be a more appropriate description." His voice sounded triumphant. "In fact, all the essentials of a fairy tale are there: 'Once upon a time, a long time ago...'" This whole idea of time is an attempt to make a ridiculous, unscientific idea seem credible. But the facts still do not line up as far as I am concerned. How can you get complex ordered systems out of disorder and chaos? Your whole theory is bankrupt!"

Never before had I had to deal with such a persistent student. My mouth was becoming dry. I was getting tired of the confrontation. As he was presenting his argument, I couldn't help but remember the "foolish" religious beliefs I had once entertained. It was obvious that Ed had been indoctrinated in the Christian belief to a far greater extent than even I had been. I remembered the narrow creationist view that I had once held before I had "honestly" evaluated the facts.

Rather than allow the argument to continue in the direction it was headed, I thought of another way this student could be put back in his place. "I can understand your tenacious attitude to hang onto your religious convictions, Ed. But, again, I must warn you that a university is no place to try and force your religious views on others. No one religion has the right to demand that their religious views be forced upon the rest of society. If you are not willing to accept the scientific view of evolution that is presented at this institution, then I would respectfully suggest that you are in the wrong field of study."

The discussion had gone on long enough with neither of us prepared to back down. It was obvious to me that the young man's opinions would not be altered. I conceded that he was entitled to his own unscientific religious views as long as he did not disturb the class and as long as they were not expressed during examination time.

"I will make the choice clear for you, Ed," I intoned

darkly, adding a parting shot with a raised eyebrow. "If you want to receive a passing grade in this course, you will be expected to answer your exam questions from the evolutionary perspective, the way you have been taught in class. The choice is up to you!"

I paused to allow my words to sink in. Ed got up and left without saying another word. I felt good, like a Boy Scout who had done his duty. I had defended the theory of evolution against yet another unenlightened thinker.

Chapter Six

GODS IN DISGUISE

"**W**hat are you doing after the briefing? Why don't you come with Sharon and me and have a drink or two?"

By now, nobody had to twist my arm to have a few drinks. That first beer I'd downed, years before at the ski lodge, had introduced me to an unhealthy habit pattern just as my father had warned. Now Jim's invitation to spend some relaxing hours at the pub brought a smile to my face.

Every Thursday afternoon, the biology lab staff gathered on campus for a weekly briefing. It was a time of preparation for the next week's classes, and afterwards it became a tradition for a group of us to stop at a favorite bar for a drink or two before heading home for supper.

This particular Thursday I was more than open to the invitation. The frustration of the day's classes had been more irksome than usual. Having a few drinks with my friends always allowed me to place the problems of everyday life on the shelf for an hour or so. Although, I hadn't spent much time thinking about it, the number of times that I could be found with a drink in my hand were becoming increasingly more frequent.

Of all the instructors that worked for me, Jim and Sharon were just a little different than the rest. Jim sported a bushy red beard and had long curly hair that hung down to the middle of his back. His unusual physical appearance, along with his untidy attire, gave him a counter cultural look. But Jim's shabby appearance was in no way related to his intellect. This American was as sharp as anyone I knew.

What really made Jim stand out from the rest of my university friends was his outspoken expression of his philosophy of life. Everyone in the biology department knew why Jim had chosen a Canadian campus to complete his graduate work. Thousands of American soldiers were losing their lives in the bloody Vietnam war and Jim had no intention of adding his name to that tragic list. To put it bluntly, Jim was also a draft dodger.

Sharon was not exactly your average student herself. About ten years older than most of the part-time instructors, Sharon was a single parent who had returned to the university to complete her degree in biology following her divorce. She was even more outspoken than Jim.

On several occasions, we had discussed topics which were of common interest. Sharon's father was a pastor of a fundamentalist, Bible-believing church and she was on a crusade against what she considered her mother and father's narrow-minded ideas.

Rather than let some of the issues remain unchallenged,

Sharon had committed herself to attack every one of her parents' beliefs.

Despite her ongoing family conflict, she was always interesting to be around. Sharon challenged my thinking in a way that no one else had done before.

That Thursday afternoon, with the briefing behind us, the three of us departed the Biology Building for "The Cavalier," or "The Cav" as we called it. The long bar, bathed in neon vapors of soft colors, was packed with students and staff. Arriving late in the afternoon usually meant that the chances of getting a seat were minimal. However, today we were fortunate. Peering through a blue haze of cigarette smoke, we spotted an empty table in a far corner. We quickly claimed it for ourselves.

"Bring us a double round of beer as quick as you can," Jim instructed the bar girl. "Looks like we've got a lot of catching up to do."

My eyes sweeping the bar, I could see what Jim meant. At the next table, a young student had passed out, his head flopped down between his knees. The sound of the Beatles' "Lucy in the Sky with Diamonds" was blasting over the juke box as a number of couples began dancing on the elevated dance area. Students behind us were laughing over the fact that they had skipped out of their afternoon classes to come to the bar, which was buzzing with activity and noise. I absently beat my leg in time with the music.

For a depressing moment, my thoughts flashed back to my childhood. Involuntarily, my father's face appeared before me and he was warning me about what happened to people who got trapped in "the alcohol habit." The combination of smoke and booze reminded me of the nauseating odor I remembered escaping through the open door of a local hometown hotel bar. As a child, I had associated it with something evil and distasteful. The same smell now penetrated my nostrils at "The Cav." A small voice from deep within me seemed to tug away at my heart and, for a moment, feelings of guilt overcame me.

Jim soon distracted me, however, as he brought us up to date on a "Peace Movement" rally that he had been putting together on campus. A number of riots had occurred on several American college campuses over the past few weeks. He had organized several noon-hour meetings in an attempt to make the Canadian students aware of what he described as "the futility of America's participation in the Vietnam war."

Just the week before, Jim had received a letter from home, informing him that his cousin had been killed in Vietnam. Although he had always been active in his antiwar efforts, this disastrous news about the death of a close relative made him even more fervent in his protest against the establishment.

Not only was Jim deeply involved in getting the student body organized to protest for peace, he was also a strong voice in the movement for a change in attitude towards ecological issues. He always made a point of drawing attention to news items reporting that the environment was being polluted. That Thursday was no exception. Jim pulled a press clipping out of his briefcase and loudly read a recent editorial, his voice competing with the sound of the noisy juke box. The article was about mercury contamination that was taking place in a number of the northern Canadian rivers.

"How much longer are we going to sit back and see the environment destroyed before we do something?" Jim asked edgily, after spending several minutes explaining the global crisis we were facing. "I can't understand why the masses can't see where we are headed! Don't you think it's time the world wakes up before it is too late?"

The looming ecological crisis was a favorite topic of discussion for me as well. I had spent many hours pondering what was going to take place in the future as the world's population continued to increase. An experiment in one of my genetics classes had focused my attention on the subject. The world faced an over-population crisis, along with the associated problems of accumulating toxic wastes. In order to demonstrate what could happen, we had placed a male and a female fruit fly in a closed container with a limited supply of nutrients. As the population of flies increased throughout the successive generations, the food supply was depleted and the waste products accumulated. At a certain point in time the population began to decline. Eventually, all the flies died.

It was obvious to me that the global human population was facing the same kind of dilemma. The only difference was that humans were capable of making choices that could bring about change. We should, for example, increase the world's food supply, control pollution and limit the birth rate.

Why was it, I wondered, that most of the people I talked to didn't seem particularly alarmed whenever I broached the subject. Most were willing to sit back and allow events to go on just as if there were nothing that could be done. Such apathy infuriated me. There had to be a solution to problems like this.

"I know exactly what you're upset about, Jim," I said, entering into the discussion. "The majority of the population senses there is a crisis facing the earth, but they believe it's too hopeless for them to personally do anything that will bring about change. It's up to people like us who are concerned to help others realize if something is not done soon, it will be too late!"

"And how do you expect to do that?" Sharon interjected. "Do you think the Biblical world view that man should have dominion over the earth will ever change here in the western world?"

"What do you mean by that?" I asked. "I'm not exactly a champion of Judeo-Christianity myself, but I don't think you can blame Christians for all the ecological problems on earth. Some of the atheistic communistic countries are less responsible about pollution than westerners."

Sharon shook her head. "You don't understand. It's not because of Christians or communists. It's because people don't understand the proper relationship between humankind and nature."

Somehow, Sharon made me feel a little defensive even though I agreed with her basic concerns. I thought she was getting off on some sort of a tangent, and I patiently explained, "I have a lot of confidence in what man can do in order to make a better earth. Look what has already been accomplished by science in just the past few decades."

"Your perspective is far too simplistic," Sharon retorted. "The problem with most of our world is that we have been programmed to believe that science has the answer for everything. As far as I am concerned, humans have far too much confidence that science will bring about a 'utopia' on this earth. Our materialistic attitudes got us into all these problems like war and pollution in the first place. There will never be peace, and the pollution of our environment will never be dealt with, until man gets a different perspective on what part he has to play on this planet.

"You've lost me, Sharon," I replied, a puzzled frown on my face. "Would you mind telling me what on earth you're talking about?"

"Certainly" she quickly replied. "Let me explain where I am coming from. You and Jim know what I believe about the traditional western religious view and how it is affecting our western society. Right?"

Sharon was always brutally outspoken about her views on Christianity. We had talked about the subject on a number of occasions. She, like myself, had come to a realization that no one religious faith should have a monopoly on the way a society should think or function. University life had shown us that there was a much broader way to look at things. It seemed so pointless that there should be hundreds of different religions, all claiming to be the "only way" to God.

Jim had been sitting back listening, and it was apparent that he was waiting for an opportunity to say something. "Well, I'll tell you what I believe," he finally chimed in, running his fingers through his long hair, "This concept that there is a personal God who decides what is good and what is bad is the biggest delusion that has ever taken place on Planet Earth. In fact, the concept that there is a God anywhere in the universe is an absolute hoax! But the thing that really bugs me," he continued, "is the idea there is a God who will 'save' us. What nonsense! The only thing that will 'save' us is the slim chance we might save ourselves if we get off our backsides and do something."

"Don't expect an argument from me, Jim," I said. "I agree with you one-hundred percent. One of the worst experiences I can remember as a kid was going to one of those high-pressure evangelical meetings and coming away feeling as if I had been beaten with a stick because I didn't walk to the front and get 'saved.'"

Whenever the opportunity arose to get into a negative discussion about religion, I always brought up what had happened to me at the evangelistic meeting I had attended in my home town.

Jim's comments had presented me with an ideal opportunity to relate the story in painful detail. In fact, each time I recounted my uncomfortable experience with the evangelist, anger welled up inside me.

"The whole concept of a personal God is a primitive belief that has always been around," I concluded, laughing sarcastically. "Some people are so weak that they need a crutch to help them limp through life. They are always trying to convert someone else to their narrow way of thinking. You are absolutely right, Jim, the future is hopeless, unless man does something constructive soon to change it."

"I can relate to the experience you went through, Roger," Sharon confided. "But don't be so negative. Would you give me a chance to explain why I believe the future does hold promise? There's hope, and it depends on a whole different way of looking at things. Will you listen to what I have to say?"

"Sure, Sharon, you're on." I was intrigued by Sharon's intense agitation. Her eyes were bright with excitement.

"Let me start by explaining that most of the ideas and beliefs we have about ourselves and others, are the result of ideas that have been forced upon us. Most of us were highly influenced, as children, by the beliefs of our parents and also by the teachers in our schools. What we don't realize is that there are other valid views about the meaning of life that we have never taken into account."

"I know what you're getting at," Jim grinned. "You've mentioned this to me before. You're talking about Eastern religions, aren't you?

"Exactly!" said Sharon. "You got it!"

"You're kidding! How did you get interested in Eastern religions"? I stared at Sharon in amazement. The conversation was taking a very different course. I ordered another beer.

"Well, actually, it was through a couple of avenues," she replied. She was obviously pleased that we were willing to hear her ideas about a topic in which she considered herself something of an expert.

"The first thing that helped open up my understanding, was a conversation I had with some Hare Krishnas," she explained. "It happened a couple of years ago, at a time when I was searching for the meaning of my own life. They seemed to have the answers to a number of questions that were bothering me.

"The other great pathway to enlightenment has been my subjects relating to Far Eastern Studies. One professor I have is a practicing Hindu. He grew up in India so he knows first-hand what Eastern religious views are all about. Between the Krishnas and my professor, I have come to understand more about life than I ever did before. In fact, there are a number of us in our class that have reached this same level of understanding."

"So what have you discovered?" I asked finally, rubbing my forehead. "Is this something I should know about?"

"That's up to you," Sharon responded, her eyes glowing. "What I can tell you, is the real difference that has taken place in my own life since I have studied some of these Hindu beliefs."

"All right, all right! Your testimonial is convincing," I interrupted. "Just tell us about what you have found out that makes so much sense to you."

"Well, the first, and most important thing, is the revelation that everything which exists is all part of a oneness in the universe. The simplest way of describing it is that 'all is one.' Everything that exists is interrelated! There is no difference between God, a human being, a potato or a rock. They are all part of a continuous reality that has no boundaries and no ultimate divisions."

"I am not sure I'm following you, Sharon. Maybe it's getting too late..." My mind didn't seem quite as sharp as usual.

"I can relate to what she is saying," Jim interjected. "This may sound crazy to you, but those exact thoughts have entered my head a number of times over the past few years, as well. But it had nothing to do with the Hare Krishnas or taking a class in Far Eastern Studies."

"That's interesting", Sharon commented. "How did it come about for you?"

"Well, I guess I'll have to admit that I have been searching for the same things you were looking for, Sharon. I knew there had to be more to this life than meets the eye. As a teenager, I rejected my parents' religious views and their assertions that there were moral absolutes. I guess I turned to science for answers to the questions I had about life. But I discovered that science and materialism didn't have all the answers either. I knew there had to be more. When I was still at high school in the States, a friend told me about an experience he had taking LSD, and how it had opened up a whole new dimension of consciousness for him. So, I decided to give it a try."

Jim's admission that he had taken LSD came as no surprise to me. In fact, on several occasions I had overheard him talking about some of his drug-related experiences to others on the campus. However, I had felt that what he was doing was his own business, just as long as his activities didn't interfere with his teaching abilities in the classroom. The drug scene was rapidly becoming commonplace on campus. I had talked with a number of people who had told me the same thing that Jim was talking about. Drugs seemed to be an avenue to open up a higher dimension of consciousness or understanding.

"So what kind of revelation did you receive?" I asked Jim.

"You probably won't understand this unless you have taken drugs yourself," Jim replied. "But the reason I brought this up is because I had experienced the same feeling of oneness with everyone and everything that Sharon is talking about, only mine occurred during an LSD experience.

"My inner-being left my body and entered another dimension beyond the physical realm. I saw the universe dissolve into vibrations. Everything was interrelated. It was the strangest feeling! It was as if I had become a minute portion of a cosmic mind, or force, which penetrated every non-living and living thing in the universe. So it became clear to me that ultimate reality is not the product of a personal God who is a separate entity or being, but everything which exists is part of God. All is God!"

"Well, I don't find that idea all that far out." I jumped into the conversation after finishing my drink. As I placed the empty glass down on the table, Jim indicated to the bar-girl we wanted another round.

"I've never had a drug experience like you have described, Jim, but I have no problem with understanding all

you have described. Why shouldn't everything be interconnected? Before the Big Bang took place, everything that
exists in this universe was together. So it's logical to accept
that all things are interrelated. We owe our very existence to
an evolutionary process which links us with the lower forms
of life and even non-living matter. If it weren't for such an
accumulation of events over billions of years, you and I
wouldn't be here to discuss what we are discussing today.
Am I right?"

"You are right about the idea that evolution ties all life
forms together," said Sharon firmly. "But there is another
aspect of evolution that also applies to what we've been
talking about. We all recognize that the evolutionary process
has produced an ever-increasing degree of complexity over
time. Life appears to be ascending towards a higher order.
We, as human beings, happen to be at the top end of the
scale. And there is no question that our destiny is already
being directed to a higher level of consciousness than the one
we're already at."

"So you think there's a next step of evolution? What do
you think it is?"

"To ascend into godhood, of course," answered Sharon.

"Godhood?" I repeated blankly.

"I believe everyone of us is a god in disguise." Sharon
continued. "The problem is, we haven't realized it yet. Only
ignorance and religious dogma keep us from attaining our
divine reality. The goal of every man, woman and child of
our generation should be to awaken the god who sleeps
within us. We must honor and worship our own being. We
must kneel to our selves. Humanity and god are one! The
sooner we, as a society, realize this, the better off we will
be, and we will understand that all knowledge and power and

truth are within each one of us. It is just waiting to be unlocked!"

"Wait a minute," I stammered. "What do you mean? This all sounds a little weird to me."

"It's not weird at all," Sharon insisted. "It's just a matter of becoming enlightened. That's all".

"Well then, how does one become enlightened?" I was becoming increasingly fascinated. "Do you suppose this could happen to me?"

"Sure it could," Sharon declared. "I don't see any reason why not. If you are really sincere about knowing more about the 'oneness' concept, I suggest that you come with me to a seminar this weekend that will be teaching some of the principles of Yoga and Transcendental Meditation. Some of the teachings of Maharishi Mahesh Yogi will be discussed. I know you'd enjoy it."

"What on earth has Yoga and T.M. got to do with all this?" I asked, genuinely puzzled.

"Wow! You certainly are still back in the dark ages, aren't you?" Sharon laughed. "Everybody knows how Yoga and T.M. add an expanded dimension to human consciousness. Some people call it 'An Altered Dimension of Awareness.' What I have been trying to tell you is, if everyone gave it a try and made an attempt to elevate their consciousness, the world would be transformed overnight. Humanity could change its direction and take a big, upward leap."

"So you are telling me that Yoga and T.M. open the door to this new awareness." Finally, I had started to see what Sharon was trying to explain to me. But, just then, the lights dimmed. It was the last call before the bar closed.

I glanced at my watch in disbelief. Where had the evening gone? I suddenly remembered that I had not even bothered to let Myrna know that I wouldn't be home for supper. Almost at the same moment, Sharon realized that she had neglected to pick up her three-year-old child from the baby sitter's after the biology lab briefing. Looking rather frustrated, Sharon got up to leave.

Thoughts of guilt flittered through my mind. We had been so busy pouring back the drinks and discussing how to change the world, that I had totally forgotten about my family. For now, I'd have to be satisfied with all I'd learned about quantum leaps of consciousness and higher levels of evolution.

At the moment the number one priority in life was to get home and face reality.

Chapter Seven

ONLY A PICKLED FETUS

My head rolled woozily on my shoulders. I squinted, clumsily trying to insert a key into the lock of the front door. It was three o'clock in the morning and all I wanted to do was to get inside and slip into bed unnoticed. As I struggled with the lock, I was unaware that I was making enough noise to wake up the dead. To my horror, the door suddenly flew open and I was confronted by the angry face of my wife. A sick, sinking feeling rose in my stomach.

"Where have you been?" she pleaded, her voice heavy with emotion and exhaustion. "Don't you have any consideration for me?" I noticed how red-rimmed her eyes looked.

I tried to form some words of apology, but my dull brain

wouldn't cooperate with my mouth. As I flopped down onto the living room couch, Myrna broke into a flood of tears.

"Can't you see what's happening to us?" By now she was weeping. "There's nothing left between us anymore. You don't even care if I exist. All you can think about is yourself."

I raised my hand to try and stem her tide of hostility. "Calm...calm down," I said, desperately trying to gather up my thoughts. "Let's just go to bed. Everything will be okay tomorrow."

Myrna, however, would not let me off the hook that easily.

"No, it's not going to be okay," she shouted. "I tried to go to sleep tonight, but I couldn't. This was the one night that I wanted you to be at home so I could talk to you. And now you come in like this. There's no use talking to you now."

Trying to pay attention, I asked my wife, a hint of resentment in my voice, "What do you want to talk about? Let's talk about it right now. What is it that's bothering you?"

Myrna worked as a nurse at the obstetrics department at the University of Saskatchewan hospital. She was employed in the delivery suite where the majority of her work dealt with delivering babies. The ward was also used for the performing of abortions. Over the past few weeks, a number of nurses had asked to be transferred to another department because they didn't want to assist in the abortions. This same issue had troubled Myrna as well, but she had not publicly protested her own feelings. In previous discussions, I had told her not to worry about it. As far as I was concerned, she had no moral obligation because "abortion was not a moral issue."

However, on this particular day, a heartbreaking scenario had taken place. An abortion that had been performed by saline procedure had resulted in a baby being aborted while it was still alive. The baby was then placed in an incubator along with the other premature infants in the hospital, where it quickly died. Seeing this whole procedure, had created an emotional dilemma, causing Myrna to lie awake, constantly rehashing the issue. She had desperately wanted to talk with me about it. I, of course, had spent the evening at a bar, solving the problems of the world.

"Myrna, we've talked about this in the past," I said, trying to form my words in a cohesive manner. "I wish you wouldn't become so emotionally distraught over such a minor issue. A fetus, while it's developing in the womb, isn't even human. It's just a blob of cells undergoing division."

Myrna had punched one of my sensitive buttons. Her words had triggered me to explode with one of my well-prepared, pro-abortion speeches.

For the past several years, I had been involved in developing a teaching aid to help students comprehend the process of cell division. As an instructor, it became apparent to me that students at the university level did not understand some of the most basic concepts of biology, one of which was mitosis or cell division. In order to help them comprehend the details regarding this very basic process necessary to the perpetuation of life, I had designed a teaching kit to visually illustrate mitosis.

At a recent biology show at the university, I had prepared a display designed to show people how cell division was essential to the development of a life, from a single cell through to the fully developed embryo. For the latter stages of the development of the embryo, I had obtained some human embryos from the University Hospital that had been preserved in formaldehyde. I had proudly displayed these specimens, my major objectives being to draw attention to the display and to demonstrate that the human embryo is a product of cell division.

"The fetus that died in the incubator was no different from the embryos I displayed in the pickle jars," I growled in a heavy voice. "So forget about this nonsense and let's go to bed."

Myrna looked at me with frightened eyes, wondering if I was even human anymore. As soon as my head hit the pillow, I was in a deep sleep. But for Myrna, the conversation about the saline abortion was just another nail in the coffin for our marriage. That night's behavior amounted to one more wedge of separation between the two of us.

The chasm was becoming wider by the day. Would there ever be a way to bridge it?

Chapter Eight

THE STING OF DEATH

Christmas with Myrna's parents had become a tradition for us. And 1973 was no different. This time we were celebrating with Myrna's two brothers, Grant and Don, who lived in Calgary. Myrna's mother and father, Tom and Ann Underschute, had joined us. Myrna stood by the illuminated Christmas tree.

She picked up a gift and handed it to our baby son, Wade, who was just nine months old. As Wade aggressively ripped the wrapping off, we all chuckled at his antics. I focused the lens of my camera on his beaming face. Then I looked across at Myrna, who was beginning to show signs that she was expecting our second child. How pretty she was, I thought to myself. The addition of children to our family had an impact on Myrna's life. She had quit her nursing position and had become a full-time mother.

We had been playing a game of Monopoly for a couple of hours, and it was getting late. I had done well as a make-believe property developer but was beginning to get tired and bored and wanted to turn in. Just then the phone rang in the kitchen. Grant left the table and picked up the receiver.

After talking for a moment, he shouted across to me, "Roger, it's for you. It's your mother."

I froze. Instantly, I knew something was wrong. Why would she be calling at 11:00 P.M. on Christmas night? We'd already talked earlier that day. I had called home to wish my parents a "Merry Christmas," and at that time Mother had told me that Dad was unable to come to the phone.

"He's resting on the living-room couch. He's under the doctor's care," she had quietly explained.

Just a few days earlier, before we had left for Calgary, I had spent the day with my parents. I had noticed a big change in my father, who was now 77 years old. When we had parted and said goodbye, there were tears in Dad's weary eyes.

"I've checked the oil in your car and added a half a quart to keep it up to full," he said, gasping for breath. "The rest of the quart is in the trunk. Make sure you keep an eye on the oil level."

This oil check was a tradition with my father. The physical effort which he had expended on this occasion had taken its toll, but, typically of Dad, he had not complained about his deteriorating health. I had looked into my father's face. Integrity was etched into every line. It was obvious, however, that something was amiss. His tired appearance and his constant shortness of breath spoke more loudly than words. I'd never known him to be sick a day in his life, so when my mother had said he couldn't come to the phone, I knew there was a serious problem.

"Roger, your Dad passed away a few minutes ago," Mother told me gently. "He died at home just before the doctor could get here."

For a long, terrible moment, I was speechless, a blank expression fixed on my face. Then I cried out, "Oh, no! not Dad!"

With great effort, I composed myself. I said, "Mom, I'll catch a plane and be there in the morning."

The shock of this news, of no longer having my Dad to talk to on the phone, was more painful than anything I had ever faced before. Childhood experiences with my father began to flood over me. I recalled sitting on his knee while he drove the tractor. The times we had spent together in the harvest fields looking at the stars. The deep, meaningful conversations we had warmly shared.

I contrasted those bonds of love Dad had given to me with the wounds I had caused him with my so-called "superior intelligence." Now it was too late to heal his heartache. Remorse gripped me; grief chilled my whole being.

Myrna came and stood by me and took my arm. She knew, by my voice, what had happened. "Your Dad's had a good life. But now he's gone to heaven," she murmured, giving me a firm hug.

Normally, I would have responded with a sarcastic comment, but now those words of comfort were my only hope. I nodded sorrowfully, then threw my arms around her and burst into tears. I continued to weep as members of her family, one by one, offered me their condolences.

That night I lay awake, staring at the ceiling, reviewing in my mind, step by step, every memory of my father that I could recapture. Myrna's words "You'll see him in heaven" echoed in my mind. I began to wonder, for the first time in years, if there was a God and if I would ever see my father again.

After a long, terrible night, morning arrived and I headed to the airport to take the plane to Saskatoon. I was picked up there by friends who drove me to the farm. My mother was waiting on the steps. It was the first time I had ever walked through the door of my parents' home without being able to greet my Dad. When I arrived, mother ushered me into the living room where several of her friends had gathered to offer their sympathy. As soon as I appeared, they got up and left, knowing that I wanted to be alone with my mother.

I sat down next to her and took her hand. I didn't know what to say so Mother took the initiative.

"Dad was proud of you," she said. Her eyes looked into mine and held me in their gaze as I wiped away the tears.

The lump in my throat choked me. I knew Dad had wanted me to be a farmer and take over the farm and so I stammered, "I guess the time has come for me to give up my job and come back to take over where he left off."

"That would be wonderful," she said softly, her face as pale as bone china. "I know that will fulfill your Dad's heart's desire."

I was coming home again, but it had taken the loss of my father to bring me back. The road of life had taken a sudden turn. And, at that moment, I could never have imagined the discovery I was about to make around the next bend.

Chapter Nine

A DAMASCUS ROAD EXPERIENCE

Snow began to whirl across the road in front of me as the windshield wiper swatted flakes as dense as goose down. I was driving Myrna back to our home on the farm from the hospital after the death of Tyler. I tightly gripped the steering wheel, but my mind was buzzing with activity. How would I ever be able to deal with this situation? I was angry and resentful. But at whom?

Why had all this happened? That was the question that kept spinning around through my mind.

Myrna touched my hand. "Life will go on," she said

softly. "We're still young. Maybe we could have another child. The doctor said that what happened with Tyler was only one chance in a thousand."

I wasn't satisfied. "But why did it happen to us?" I said, lashing out bitterly, although not at her. "I don't understand."

The snow continued to collide with the windshield and I peered through it, searching the road ahead for obstacles. Suddenly, something unprecedented and extraordinary occurred. Without hearing an audible voice, and with a powerful sensation of being enveloped by a blanket of love, thoughts began to formulate in my mind with absolute clarity.

"The death of your child has happened for a reason: to change the course of your life. Just as you are headed down this road, Roger, so you are on the road of life. But as for that road, you're going in the wrong direction. It's time to stop and turn around."

Then a second distinct message came into my mind: "Think less about yourself and more about how you can help others."

Without saying a word, I glanced out of the corner of my eye to see if Myrna was experiencing the same sensation that I was. She obviously wasn't and continued to stare out of the front window, as if mesmerized by the windshield wipers swiping away at the driving snow.

Even though it had been a painful situation for us to lose our child, we at least wouldn't have to experience the life-long burden of bringing up a handicapped child. I thought about those parents who have to do that, and for the first time in my life, I began to feel sorry for them and to understand a little of how they must feel. An unexpected thought came to me, "Perhaps there's a way that I could help them." It was as if my mind were suspended in time and space.

"I don't understand what's happening," I blurted out to Myrna. "I've never experienced anything like this before."

Myrna's eyes left the road ahead and looked at me quizzically. "Roger, what are you talking about?"

I tried to explain what had occurred during the last few minutes as those uninvited thoughts had rushed through my mind as if I were watching a big-screen T.V. in Times Square, New York. "Maybe this has happened so that I won't be so selfish and will become more concerned about others," I said. "Maybe this is a pivotal point in my life."

In making that statement, I had admitted to myself for the first time ever, that I had staged a big show on the outside, but inside I was really hurting. My life was just a facade.

When we arrived back at the farm, we walked into our house to be greeted by our boys, aged four and five, and Myrna's parents, who were looking after them. Everyone was quiet.

"You're brother's gone to heaven," Myrna told our sons.

Normally, I would have lashed out angrily at such a comment, but now, after what had occurred in the car, I almost wanted to agree.

We put the boys to bed and gave them comforting hugs. "Everything's going to be okay," I told them.

About two weeks later, I was asked to become the chairman of The Eston World Gopher Derby, a fund-raising project for the needs of the handicapped sponsored by the Eston Lions Club, of which I was a member. My first thought was that I didn't have time. Then I recalled the vivid experience that I'd had on the road back from the hospital.

"Think less about yourself and more about how you can help others," were the words that had stuck in my mind.

Perhaps, I reasoned, this was exactly what was necessary to get my mind off of myself.

The project had become noted throughout Western Canada as an annual event associated with the Dominion Day holiday of July 1. A race track was designed with eight racing lanes, each stacked one on top of the other. Gophers, squirrel-like prairie rodents that are plentiful throughout Western Canada, raced down the lanes, competing for the championship. When the gate was pulled, the gophers scurried down the track towards a hole, which was actually a tubular can. The first one to dive into the can mechanically tripped a flag, which indicated the winner.

My mind started to become active with ideas on how the World Gopher Derby could become a vehicle to raise funds to help those specially concerned with the needs of the handicapped. As I worked on the Derby, I began to notice a change in my own personality. The more time and energy I spent on thinking about others, the less time I had to think about myself. And I liked the changes that were occurring in my personality.

At the same time, some other thoughts were coming to me on a frequent basis. Alcohol was a major factor in the deterioration of my relationship with my wife and family. It became apparent to me that it not only affected me negatively, but also others who used it. I would sometimes get together with my friends and would become uncomfortable with the whole lifestyle associated with drinking. It was becoming abundantly clear that there was nothing good about drinking. Every aspect of it was negative.

On New Year's Eve, 1977, Myrna and I went to a party

and I didn't take a single alcoholic drink. "Maybe I can begin the New Year turning over a new leaf," I thought, as I entered the front door of our home. I slipped into the bedroom, making sure that no one saw me, and knelt down beside my bed. For the first time since I was a teenager, I uttered a prayer.

"God, if you exist, help me to keep this New Year's resolution. I want to give up drinking."

After having been in bondage to alcohol for ten years, it was a big step. I had tried several times before to make a similar resolution on my own, it had never worked out. So a prayer like this, to a God in whom I didn't even believe, was the ultimate act of surrender.

Several days later, I noticed that I no longer had a desire to drink. I went to our liquor cupboard and poured the bottles of rum and vodka down the sink.

With alcohol consumption removed from my daily activities, I had much more time to spend at home with my family. Although I still continued to curl competitively, as soon as the games were over, I headed home rather than to the bar. Soon my friends began to notice the change that had occurred in my life.

"Oak, are you on the wagon?" one fellow curler inquired.

"I'm on a diet," I said, not really wanting to admit that I had totally given up alcohol. But it didn't take long for everyone to see that the changes were not for dietary purposes, but were the beginning of a new life for Myrna and me.

As my mind began to return to normal, the world around me seemed to be much more interesting and colorful. I had time at home to be with my family. After they had gone to bed, I began to read and learn in real earnest.

One evening, I'd been sitting on the couch deeply engrossed in a biology textbook. I set it down to watch the 10 o'clock news. I started to glance around the room during a commercial break, and I absently looked at the wall and saw a painting that had hung there as long as I could remember. A simple thought passed through my mind, "That picture was painted by an artist.

I looked down at the table in front of me. I had made that table in woodworking class in high school.

Then I looked at the book on the table and the thought came clearly to me, This book was written by an author. I opened the book and saw a diagram of a cell. And the thought came clearly to my attention: If paintings have artists, tables have carpenters and books have authors, then what about living things? Life is far more complex! How could it have originated without a designer?

I gasped, recognizing the profound impact this simple idea was about to have on my thinking. The idea that life had to be created or designed went totally against all that I had believed and taught as a biology instructor. If life had been created, then what about evolution?

For a moment, I tried to reason this revolutionary concept out of my mind. If life was created and there was a Creator, then why are there so many mistakes? I thought back to our own child who had been born severely malformed and imperfect.

With that unanswered, I pushed my new questions aside and went to bed. Perhaps this was just a passing phase that would go away.

The next few days, an interesting phenomenon occurred in my thinking. I was constantly confronted with ideas and thoughts of opposite meaning. I started to recognize that, as an individual, I had the option to make certain choices. I could be forgiving or unforgiving. I could be proud or humble. I could show love or show hatred. It was up to me - the choice was mine.

As I attempted to willfully choose to be a more caring person, I started to experience a complete personality change. It even became apparent to my friends and family that something was happening to me that was transforming my life. One day, while sitting in my living room, I decided to analyze the changes that had been taking place in my life over the past few weeks. I began to list what I called my new philosophy of life, the various changes and ideas that had occurred. Taking a pen, I wrote, point by point:

1) Care about others rather than yourself.

2) Love, forgive, and be humble.

3) Life is better explained by creation than by evolution.

Then I began to understand why my mind was still in turmoil. Suppose, in the beginning, there had been a Creator and things had been perfect. But then, somehow, something had occurred to affect this perfect creation. Things were no longer perfect. It seemed as if there were a struggle between good and evil, between God and some other force. Was I caught in the middle of a spiritual battle?

After laying out this new philosophy and re-reading the points, it all seemed strangely familiar. I had, at one time, believed all of this before.

As I contemplated these points, my mind exploded with activity. "Wow, I can't believe it! These are Biblical principles!" I shouted, jumping up off the chair. "What have I been doing over these years? How could I have missed this? There must be a God. There was a creation! And there must be a devil, who is God's adversary!"

Myrna popped her head in from the kitchen and asked, "Who are you talking to?"

I smiled. "You're going to think I'm crazy, but I've just come to the most incredible revelation of my entire life," I told her. "The Bible--it's true!"

At this point, Myrna didn't know what to think. I was constantly getting enthused about something or other and then the excitement would die down. I was zealous about whatever I did. Was this just another phase I was passing through? She couldn't help but wonder.

I went out to a nearby Christian bookstore and bought a Bible story book for my boys. I started reading the stories to them. As I did, the Bible started to become alive to me. It was more interesting to me than to them. Suddenly, I had the faith of a little child.

"There was a flood and the world was destroyed," I would say incredulously, "Noah was a real person! And Adam and Eve really lived."

Somewhere in my library I located, *The Late Great Planet Earth* by Hal Lindsey and re-read it. This time it made sense--Bible prophecy and its connection with current events fascinated me.

One night several weeks later, after recognizing that the Bible was an authentic book inspired by Almighty God, I became frustrated. I had been trying to live a lifestyle that I thought would be pleasing to God. I was endeavoring to be humble and loving and kind, but I had to come to the realization that none of this would be enough. God was perfect and holy. I was not, nor could I ever be, no matter how hard I tried.

What can I ever do that will make me acceptable to God? I puzzled over the question. I knew that I had made some changes in the right direction, but those efforts were not good enough. No matter how I looked at it, God was perfect. I wasn't.

Myrna sat opposite me as I said out loud, "I don't understand why a perfect God, who's allowed the world to become imperfect, would let life go on. Why am I here? God, why do you let me exist?"

There was absolute silence and then, without a voice booming out of heaven or writing appearing on the wall, a thought became engraved on my mind; *"You've come to believe in the Bible, then believe what the Bible says about Christmas, Easter, the birth, the death and the resurrection of Jesus Christ. The way has already been provided so that you can have a relationship with the Creator for eternity.*

"Believe what the Bible has to say about Jesus Christ."

I leaped to my feet. I almost ran to a nearby bookshelf and grabbed my old Bible. I had been ten years old when my parents had given it to me as a birthday present. My father had written a verse inside the cover. I read the verse, and, for the first time in my life, John 3:16 meant something to me.

> *For God so loved the world,*
> *That He gave his only begotten Son,*
> *That whosoever believes in Him*
> *Should not perish*
> *But have everlasting life.*

I was breathless. It was as if I had opened a door and walked into a new room. Jesus Christ was a real person. He was the Son of God. He had lived a perfect life for me. All I had to do was to believe. The verse that I had memorized as a child, over twenty years before, was true.

I turned to my wife and said, "How could I possibly have missed this? It's incredible! Do you believe in Jesus as the way to eternal life?"

She nodded. "Yes, Roger, I've believed that since I was a little girl," she said. "In fact, I can remember the day I went to a Sunday School class with one of my friends and prayed with the Sunday School teacher."

At that moment, Myrna walked away into our bedroom and came back holding a plaque in her hands. "This is the plaque that they gave me that day," she said.

I was stunned as she read out loud the verse John, chapter three, verse sixteen. "For God so loved the world, that He gave..."

God had given His Son's life for me nearly two thousand years before. Just as I had rejected my own father's gift of spiritual truth for most of my lifetime I had also rejected my Heavenly Father's gift of salvation. Now, at last, I understood. The deception which had clouded my life for years was dispelled.

After nearly three decades of living, my life had finally begun. Just as the scriptures promised, old things had passed away. And behold--I, and all things pertaining to me and my existence on earth, had immediately and irreversibly become new.

Chapter Ten

CALLED TO WITNESS

"It's time to go to bed," Myrna yawned loudly as the clock struck twelve. "Aren't you going to put the Bible down and get some sleep?"

In a couple of exhilarating days, I had almost devoured Matthew, Mark Luke and John, reading them as if they had been penned specifically for me. I'd started into the book of Acts and a particular verse appeared to jump out at me from the page. It quoted the last words Jesus said before the Ascension, "...you shall be my witnesses in Jerusalem and in all Judea and Samaria and to the end of the earth."

I read the verse over and over again. Although I recognized that these were words Jesus had specifically proclaimed to those who were gathered around Him before He ascended into heaven, it seemed as if I, too, had been selected, at this time, to hear them as well. I was overwhelmed that I had wasted so many years. Was there something I could do now to proclaim to others my new-found belief in Jesus Christ? Could I really be a witness?

Doubt soon filled my mind. This must be my imagination. Who am I and who would even believe me? I don't know much about the Bible. I'm just a farmer. Who would believe a farmer? But the impression was so strong that I couldn't deny it.

I sensed that whatever I was to do related to my former biology background at the university. I was being called to proclaim the reality of the Bible. The message would be heard far and wide and would be simple and easy to understand.

Myrna's voice broke into my thoughts again, asking me to come to bed. "Sit down for a moment," I asked her.

"There's something I want to talk to you about. This may seem strange, but as I've been reading this particular verse, I feel like God is calling me to proclaim my faith to others, here at home first of all, then the surrounding area and finally around the world."

I repeated my thoughts out loud, especially questioning how I, a farmer, would ever get a hearing. I was greatly relieved when she smiled.

"I don't find that totally impossible," she said.

"You don't? Why did you say that?"

"Do you remember the book that I was reading in the hospital that made you so angry."

I nodded. "I remember. It was called **The Road to Bythinia** and it was about the life of Luke."

She smiled again. "I remember a part of that book where Luke was questioning his call or mission and he had similar concerns, just as you've expressed. And look how God used him!"

Myrna quickly located the book and flicked through it, trying to find a particular page.

I told her I would read it through for myself, and the next night I began enthusiastically. When I got to this particular portion of the book she was talking about, my thoughts were confirmed. Yes, God could use ordinary people to proclaim his truth. And, without a doubt, this time He had really chosen one.

The first step towards my Biblical training was for me to go to church. Up until this point in time, I'd been dropping off the boys at the local United Church of Canada Sunday School and picking them up afterwards. The following Sunday, I decided it would be good for our whole family to attend church. I couldn't remember the last time I had been in a Sunday morning service. I guessed it must have been with Mom and Dad when I was a teenager.

I was excited when the minister stood up in the pulpit to give the message. But, shortly after he began to speak, I became confused. He described the Genesis account of creation as an allegory, or "mytho-poetic." He explained to the congregation that the real account of origins could be "better explained scientifically." I couldn't comprehend what I was hearing.

At the end of the service, along with the rest of the congregation, I stood in line to shake hands with the minister. I waited until most of the people had left. There were two items I wanted to cover with him. First of all, I wished to apologize to him for my rude behavior when he had come to our home expressing sympathy for the loss of our baby. At that point I was uncomfortable with his presence and was rather short with him. I also wanted to clarify what he was trying to say in his message.

As we shook hands, I asked the minister if I could spend some time in private with him and he agreed to meet me later that day in his office. I went at the appointed time and, with great excitement, I began to share about the changes that had taken place in my life since we'd last met.

"You'll never believe what's happened to me," I enthusiastically. "In fact, I don't even know how to describe it. It's like I've come into some kind of a spiritual awakening."

He looked puzzled. "What do you mean? What's happened to you?"

My eyes ablaze with excitement, I explained, "For so many years, I rejected the Bible as nonsense, but over the past several months, I've come to realize that it is really the truth.

I was surprised to find that he didn't share my enthusiasm. "Oh, that's nice," he said, looking at me suspiciously. "I'm glad that you've been comforted after your recent loss."

After a few moments of strained silence, I went on to tell him the real reason I was there. I asked him to explain what he meant by his comments regarding the Biblical creation account being a "myth." The minister enlarged upon the explanation he'd given during the morning service, declaring science as "the authority" on the subject, not the Bible.

I was genuinely bewildered. "The reason I became a Christian is because I've come to believe the Biblical account of creation," I told him. "It's become crystal clear in my thinking that the whole idea of evolution is just a deception of Satan."

The cleric coughed and looked at me warily over his glasses. There was an uncomfortable pause, and then he spoke. "Satan?" he repeated incredulously. "Where did you come up with that idea?" After a pause, he added, "I think the stress you have been through has caused you some emotional trauma, Roger. You mean to tell me that you are willing to toss out all of your years of university education, to reject what scientists have proven to be true, and to accept the Biblical account literally?"

I was stunned. I felt as if my heart was about to explode. For a moment I questioned whether he was right and I was wrong. I couldn't argue or debate with him because I didn't have the biblical knowledge that I needed. But I knew that what had happened to me was real. My life had changed and nobody could deny that.

"I guess I'm in the wrong place," I said, a hint of sadness in my voice. I got up, and shook his hand, saying, "Maybe some day I'll be able to explain." I told him. "Some day, somewhere, sometime, you'll remember this discussion." I was devastated. I had to get away and think.

I stood up and smiled weakly. "I can't prove that I'm right, but I know that you're wrong!"

As I found my way out of his office in a daze, my whole body trembling, I wondered if maybe I really had lost my grip on reality.

At home, I didn't tell Myrna about the disturbing discussion. I felt I had been rolled over by a steam engine. I wanted to find someone I could talk to--someone who would really understand where I was coming from.

All at once, I thought of the Reverend G.S. McLean, the pastor who had preached at my father's funeral. Dad had stopped going to the United Church for the previous ten years because of what he called the "liberal theology" of the pastor. Occasionally, however, he would go to the local Full Gospel church. So, when he died, I wanted to have G.S. McLean, a retired pastor, a friend of my father, give the sermon at the funeral.

"This is a man," I thought, "who may understand what has happened to me." I recalled that the sermon at my father's funeral had been based on John 3:16. Summoning my courage, I went to his house and knocked on the door. His wife, Hazel, greeted me and invited me to sit down at the kitchen table until he returned home. He was teaching a class at the Full Gospel Bible Institute in Eston, a school founded in the 1940s to train young people to be Bible teachers and missionaries. Pastor McLean was the founding president and had also been pastor of the local church for almost forty years.

In a few minutes he arrived home. A small, spritely gentleman in his sixties, with heavy black glasses and peppery hair, he was surprised to see me. The last time we had talked together was the day of my Dad's funeral, which had taken place four-and-a-half years before.

"Roger, how good it is to see you again!" he exclaimed as he took off his heavy overcoat, scarf and hat. He sat down across the kitchen table from me. His engaging attitude immediately put me at ease.

"I've come here because I have some questions. There are some issues I want to talk to you about," I started. "I'm not sure how I should begin or what I should say. But some changes have taken place in my life and I'm having difficulty understanding what has happened to me."

He looked intently at me. "Go on, Roger, tell me."

"It's like I've had some kind of awakening," I said. "It's

as if I'm beginning a new life. The Bible has become alive to me. This book," I said pointing to a Bible that was lying in front of us, "is really true."

"Yes, yes, go on. Tell me more," he said, looking intently at my flushed face.

"Okay, I will, but promise me you won't laugh if I do," I said, still bruised from my meeting with the United Church of Canada minister. McLean indicated with a nod that he wouldn't laugh, so I pressed on.

"Here's what I have come to believe: there is a God, there was a creation, there was an Adam and Eve. Something happened to the perfect creation. There was a global flood, and I believe that what the Bible says about the future is really going to happen. But what has become most real to me is that now I know Jesus Christ really died for my sins. When I came to that understanding, my life totally changed."

There was silence for a few seconds as I waited breathlessly for his response. A big smile broke out on his face. When I glanced at his wife Hazel, she was also grinning from ear to ear.

"What has happened to you, Roger, is that God's hand of grace is upon your life," he said finally. "And it is real! What has happened to you is an answer to prayer. Both my wife and I have been praying for you ever since your Dad died because we sensed that you were seeking for the truth."

"Really?" I was astonished. "You were praying for me?"

After he and Hazel had assured me of their intercession on my behalf, I explained that there was something else I wanted to discuss with him. I went on to say that I was feeling a bit reluctant about it.

He responded with great sincerity. "I want to hear

whatever it is you have to say, Roger."

And so I plunged in. "This may sound crazy to you, and I don't know how to explain it, but I feel like all this has happened to me for a reason. I believe that God has changed my life because he wants to use me to speak to people about the truth all over the world. It sounds so ridiculous, I don't know if it's my own imagination, or if it's real."

G.S. picked up the Bible in front of him and said, "This book is filled with stories about men and women God used in incredible ways so that He could receive the glory. So what you're feeling, Roger, is well within the realm of possibility."

I sighed a breath of relief and tears began to streak down my cheeks.

As I recovered my composure, I told him, "My mind is so full of evolution. I know it isn't true, but I don't know how to explain some of these concepts that I have accepted."

I fired scores of questions at him, issues that I had been unable to resolve relating the Bible to some of the things I had studied at the university. I asked him what he knew about creation and evolution. In five minutes, he spoke more truth than I had heard in my entire life. I sat there astounded, almost breathless.

Then I asked one very essential question: how could I find out more about how Bible and true science agree?

To my continuing amazement, he told me that he taught a seminar on this very subject. The audio tapes of that seminar were available at the Bible School. "Why don't you get the tapes and listen to them?" he said. "Then come back, once you've heard them, and we'll talk some more."

I drove straight to the school and picked up the tapes before I went home. That night Myrna and I started to listen to G. S. McLean's lectures. I could hardly believe the information I was hearing and how fascinating the subject matter was. The very things he was talking about--facts that support the Biblical principles of creation--profoundly confronted the evolutionary world view. They were revolutionary.

As one tape concluded, I quickly popped it out and then put another in. The whole series took six hours and I went right through from start to finish. I just couldn't believe that this man, with this information, lived in our community.

As I spent more time researching the scriptures and talking to others about the subject, it became apparent that my friends and I were going in opposite directions. My former drinking buddies were saying, "Oakland's got religion and he's lost touch with reality." It seemed as if no one wanted to get close to Myrna and me.

Most people thought the reason I had become so religious was the loss of our child. People concluded that it was just a passing phase that would soon be over. Eventually I'd get my feet back on the ground. When Myrna became pregnant with our fourth child, the consensus was that after the baby was born, I'd get back to being my old self again.

We both knew that this baby Myrna was carrying was a special gift from God. During the summer, tests were done and we learned that it was going to be a girl. The birth was scheduled for the end of November, just a little over a year after the day Tyler died.

On November 25, 1978, Angela Jean was born. This was the first time I had mustered enough courage to be there for the birth of one of our children. What a dramatic and moving experience it was for me!

In a little over a year, Myrna and I had seen one life

snatched from us and another given. My wife held the baby on her chest and I held her hand. Looking at our daughter's perfect features, we thanked God together for the miraculous change that had occurred in our lives in a little over a year. It was as if God had used the death of Tyler to give new life to all of us.

Although the other children were special, this was the first child's birth for which we gave God all the glory. My witness became even more apparent to the people that knew me. Instead of having my feet on the ground, I was now ten feet in the air.

It became more and more difficult to participate in the same social functions I had attended in the past. One day one of my friends called me aside and said he wanted to talk to me. "Roger," he said, "I don't know what's happened to you. You've done a complete 180 degree turn. It's as if your life has totally changed direction."

I looked at him, and then responded. "You're right. I have changed directions. The reason is that I'm following a new Leader. I hope some day you'll understand."

From that moment on, Myrna and I began to pray intensely for our friends, that God's grace would begin to work in their lives the way it had in ours.

Chapter Eleven

THE OAKLAND RAIDERS

For a moment, I was transported back to the high school auditorium where I had been so put off by Christianity. Now another voice behind another pulpit was making the same demand for me to "come forward and publicly make a stand for Jesus Christ." I winced for a moment as I remembered the lady who had tapped me on the shoulder and shouted, "Son, you must go to the front. You don't want to burn in hell, do you?"

It was January 7, 1979. That Sunday afternoon, I had gone to visit Myrna's aunt and uncle, Cliff and Lois Underschute, because I wanted to tell them about the spiritual changes taking place in my life. They had told us that they would pray for us before Myrna went to the hospital to give birth to Tyler. Now I needed to tell them the whole story, since they had heard rumors that something was happening in our lives.

I rang the bell of their two-bedroom bungalow. Cliff, a retired grain superintendent, greeted me at the door. "Come on in," he said, in his usual friendly fashion. "Take a chair."

After spending a few minutes talking about farming, I brought up the real reason I was there. I related to them, step-by-step, the process that had brought me to the reality of Jesus Christ. I explained how I had come to realize that evolution was not true and that I was now a Biblical creationist. They were amazed as I unfolded my story.

"Your prayers for Myrna and me were answered," I told them. Following a time of praying together, Cliff told me about a meeting that was scheduled at their church that evening.

"An evangelist by the name of Alf Rees is speaking tonight." said Cliff. "Why don't you come with us?" These were special meetings to be held for the Bible School students as their second term was beginning. As was customary, the community-at-large was invited.

The snow crunched beneath our feet as we got out of the warm car and made our way along the icy sidewalk to the church. It was a typical 40-degree-below-zero night in Saskatchewan. The last time I had entered this white stucco building had been the day my father was buried. I took off my coat and put it on a peg alongside scores of others.

The place was packed and I nervously looked around to see if I knew anyone there. I could see surprise at my unexpected appearance written across several familiar faces in the congregation .

For the first part of the service, a choir sang. I thought

the roof was going to come off, they sang with such gusto. It became so hot inside that the ushers had to open the windows to allow some of the frigid outside air to cool the place down. We were jammed in like sardines.

At the end of the worship service, the main speaker, Alf Rees, came to the pulpit. In contrast to the evangelist that had so turned me off as a child, this man spoke with authority, not theatrics.

"I came here tonight with a prepared message," he began in a deep, baritone voice. "But God has impressed upon me that I should make a change. So the sermon for tonight is going to be called, *'Are you a history reader or a history maker?'*"

Briefly, I wondered what this had to do with the Bible. But, as he proceeded to lay out the Biblical scenario of how God used "unusual and unlikely characters" to perform His plan, his message cut directly into my heart. Over and over again, he repeated "Jesus said, 'Follow me and I will make you fishers of men.'" Each time he said it, he stared at the congregation. And each time he stared at the congregation, I thought he was looking directly at me.

The message concluded with a challenge. "There are people here tonight who need to make a decision," he said. "Who are you going to follow? I am going to challenge you to make the decision to follow Christ by getting up out of your seat and walking to the front."

My heart sank into my stomach. In fact, it almost seemed as if it stopped beating a couple of times. I wondered if I should rush out the back door as I had done sixteen years before, or respond to his challenge and walk courageously up to the front.

I knew if I did, living in a small town, that there would be no turning back. My commitment to Jesus Christ would be known everywhere.

Fortunately, this time the right decision wasn't hard to make. I rose to my feet, walked to the front and fell to my knees.

I'd finally stopped running from God.

Just over a month later, I stood nervously before my first-ever audience at the Free Methodist Church in Avon Lee, Saskatchewan. Twelve hardy souls stared back at me. I had been introduced to them, that day in February 1979, by G.S. McLean, who had already delivered his presentation.

"With me tonight," he said, "is Roger Oakland, a former biology instructor at the University of Saskatchewan, who was once committed to evolution. He has now become a Biblical creationist, and he's going to share a few words with you this evening."

It was my first chance to speak publicly on the creation-evolution controversy. Not suspecting that there would be any opposition in a small church in a tiny prairie community, I felt this was a good place to begin my creationist career.

For several minutes I explained why I had changed my commitment from evolution to creation. In the back row I could see a young lady who was getting particularly agitated, as if she were anxious to say something. Suddenly, she stood to her feet and began to challenge me.

"This is sheer nonsense!" she declared, with real venom in her voice. "You might be able to hoodwink these people who have never had an education, but I'm here to tell you that I won't be fooled. I'm the high school biology teacher in this community." She looked around as if expecting to receive plaudits from the group for her stand.

Several of the older members of the congregation looked away, embarrassed.

"I was invited here by one of my students who attends this church," she pressed on. "I'm sorry to say, Mr. Oakland, that these foolish arguments for your faith don't impress me."

Her zealous defense of evolutionary beliefs reminded me of my own behavior when I was defending evolution at the university. It was hard to believe that I was now in an opposite role.

I studied her angry face. "If you are comfortable in believing what you believe without fairly examining the evidence," I responded, "then, that's entirely up to you. That's your choice. I can empathize with you--I know exactly how you must feel. But I challenge you to open up your mind and think for a few moments. Much of what you're defending is not based on solid evidence. You've simply believed what you've been told."

To my surprise, she stopped her tirade and sat down. In fact, she remained to the end of the meeting and then left hastily, before the pastor could finish his closing prayer.

On the 250 mile drive back to Eston the next day, I turned to G.S. McLean and asked him what he thought of the confrontation. "Have you often been challenged in your meetings the way I was last night?"

With his eye on the road ahead and his hand on the wheel, he responded, "It's important for you to understand, Roger, that truth often brings confrontation, and sometimes even emotional hostility. But don't be thrown off track by that kind of response.

When a person becomes hostile, his initial reaction isn't necessarily a true measure of what his final response will be.

You just have to plant the seeds and leave the rest up to the Lord."

Later that year, Pastor McLean was invited to attend a science curriculum meeting that would determine whether or not the subject of creation could be taught in the public schools. A number of concerned parents had expressed the desire to see creation presented alongside evolution in the curriculum. I went as an observer. For several hours, in front of department heads of biology, my friend presented a creation world view, contrasting it with the theory of evolution. In the concluding remarks, the university professors were extremely dismissive and rude in their assessment of what he had said.

They refused to examine with an open mind the evidence he presented. I was distraught by their response, naively thinking that his presentation would have changed their thinking. Part of the presentation had included a number of fossils that, to me, clearly revealed that life had been destroyed in the past by volcanic destruction, which agreed with the Biblical perspective. Those "experts" refused even to look at them. As I was gathering up the fossils and putting them away in boxes, a janitor walked into the room to see what was going on.

He picked one of the fossils up, and asked. "How come you've got all these rocks here?"

"They're not rocks," I answered. "They're fossils."

"What's a fossil? I'm only a janitor. You'll have to explain."

"Fossils are the preserved remains of creatures that were destroyed in the past." I told him.

"So, what's that got to do with the biology department?"

Trying to simplify the subject, I said, "These fossils represent living things that were destroyed by a global catastrophe. We were here to give a presentation on Biblical creation."

"What kind of global destruction are you talking about?" he said in a thick, Ukrainian accent. "Do you mean Noah's flood?"

"Yes," I smiled, "that's right. Noah's flood."

"You mean," he was starting to become excited, "that there's actual evidence to support the Bible? Nobody's every told me that before."

For the next several minutes, the janitor enthusiastically listened as I showed him what we had come there to present to the closed-minded intellectuals.

The irony struck me. We'd come to try and convince the men at the top that they were wrong and had failed hopelessly. But a janitor with an open mind had listened. All at once I knew that I had been called to communicate my message to janitors, farmers, and fishermen. I was to present my message to the common man because he hadn't yet closed his mind to the truth about creation and the Creator.

During the following months, requests for Pastor McLean's seminar continued to come in from throughout Western Canada. I started to travel with him extensively and participate with him as a seminar speaker. It became apparent that the opportunities were more than the two of us could handle. It was becoming a full-time job.

It was difficult to fulfill my responsibilities both on the farm and as a speaker. I invited Larry McLean, the son of Pastor McLean and a police officer in Calgary, Alberta, to help both on the farm and in our seminar team. Together, we researched and developed audio-visual materials and expanded the whole subject matter into a seminar called, *The*

Bible, Key to Understanding Science, History, and the Future. As tapes and videos were distributed, invitations poured in, not only from throughout Canada, but from other parts of the world as well.

However, it was in my own backyard that the most extraordinary thing happened. In June of 1981, a friend of mine backed his pick-up truck over his two-year-old daughter. She was killed in this tragic accident and the couple, Ed and Ruth, were stricken with grief. Myrna and I were able to comfort them by sharing our faith in Jesus Christ, helping them see how God had worked in our lives through the loss of our own child.

Through this tragedy, Ed and Ruth's new-found faith was demonstrated to the community. Later on, several of our friends requested that we gather together in a home one evening. They wanted me to explain why I believed the Bible was true.

One Saturday evening, over a period of several hours, Larry McLean and I presented portions of our seminar to show physical, observable evidence that agreed with the Biblical world view. Following this, several other opportunities arose and friends gathered in other homes. Before the end of the summer, more than fifteen couples who hadn't attended church for years started to go to church. One by one, they publicly made commitments to the Lordship of Jesus Christ.

This group of on-fire Christians, who shared their faith with everyone they could, came to be known as "The Oakland Raiders." Obviously, their leader wasn't a man named Oakland, however. They may have been influenced by me, but they were serving Jesus Christ.

Myrna and I had asked God to enable us to witness to our

friends. And the prayers we had so fervently offered for that cause had been answered. The fulfillment of God's call on our lives had begun. Where would He take us next?

Chapter Twelve

"GO TELL IT ON THE MOUNTAIN"

There wasn't too much Christmas "spirit" at the Mall. Or, maybe there was too much spirit flowing. People were shoving and pushing each other to get to the front of the line to purchase their Yuletide "bargains." Suddenly a scuffle broke out in a store I was passing.

"Hey, buddy, don't try and jump the line. I was here before you!" shouted an inebriated shopper as he angrily grabbed a man by the back of his overcoat. "Get to the back of the line where you belong!"

In that Calgary shopping center a few days before Christmas, 1984, I looked around in disgust. Myrna and I were there to do some last-minute shopping for our family.

Upon our arrival at the mall, we had agreed to go our separate ways, and to meet later at a specific place. Even before the shouting incident occurred, it had been obvious to me that the vast majority of Christmas shoppers didn't have a clue about the real meaning of the season.

I completed my last purchase, a computer game from Radio Shack for the boys, and was on my way to meet Myrna at the main entrance to the Mall. Just then, above the noise of the people that were shuffling and chattering around the mall, I heard the sweet sound of a choir.

No one else seemed to be aware of the beautiful music that was drifting from the second floor balcony. I stopped to listen more intently to what the choir was singing.

"Go tell it on the mountain...that Jesus Christ is born."

I was transfixed. As I stood there alone, I realized that the message of Jesus Christ, which was what Christmas was supposed to be all about, was being ignored. The world had been deceived about the message of Jesus Christ and why He had come to earth. Even Canadians were not paying attention to this "Good News." There were people all over the world who had not even heard about Jesus Christ. But here in my own homeland, nearly everyone had heard, but nobody was listening.

Memory carried me back to the time I had read in Acts 26, how the Apostle Paul was called in Christ's service on the road to Damascus. I had read and reread these verses shortly after becoming a believer, and the words that were spoken by Jesus to Paul [then known as Saul], had made a profound impression on me.

Now, listening to the Christmas choir, I knew beyond a

shadow of doubt that God had appointed me to be a "minister and a witness." He was reconfirming my calling to share my faith about the reality of Jesus Christ around the world. My calling and mission was clear: to turn unbelievers from "darkness to light".

A few minutes later, not quite on time, I saw my wife rushing towards me through the crowd with some bags in her hands. "Did you get all of the things that you wanted?" I asked.

"It's almost impossible to get anything here," she said. "I can't believe the way people are behaving. Let's go!"

As we started toward the exit, she suddenly exclaimed, "Roger, did you hear the choir singing?"

I told her with excitement what I had experienced as I'd listened to the words. She breathlessly explained that she had heard the song and had the same feeling. We both walked towards the car without another word to each other. There was nothing more to say. We were both fully aware that we'd just shared a divine appointment with the Lord.

In the days and months to follow, opportunities to speak at seminars and conferences increased, coming to us from many different parts of the United States and Canada. The Bible and Science Department expanded as a good friend of mine, Doug Schneider, joined the team. Doug and his wife, Heather, were among the couples who had come to the Lord during the Eston revival. Now both of them had become involved in full-time ministry. Doug had sold his share in a farm machinery dealership and had established the Bible School's video production department. The outreach, through the production and distribution of audio and video tapes, was beginning to reach people in many parts of the world.

In February of 1985, Pastor McLean, Larry McLean and

I were asked to hold a seminar in the Koloa Church on the island of Kauai. At the end of the first evening, a man came up to talk to me. His name was Richard Hughes, and he was a businessman from British Columbia, Canada.

"The information you presented tonight should be the content for a film," he said. "Would you be interested in working together on a project that would expose the fallacy of evolution?"

I nodded in a non-committal way, not wanting to get too excited about Mr. Hughes' idea. But when he came back a second, third, and finally the fourth night, asking to meet with our team, it became clear that he was serious about his proposal. He had a deep desire to see such a project undertaken.

He explained to us that he had been involved in the production of several Christian film documentaries, such as *The God Makers* and *Gods of the New Age*. As we sat around the table at our hotel, Richard suggested that we outline a script for a film documentary which would expose evolution and, at the same time, present a biblical world view.

I returned to Saskatchewan and began gathering further research materials for such a film. During this process a number of insights began to emerge in my thinking which further clarified the profound impact evolution was having on society. Not only had evolution been Satan's device to make mankind question the reality of the Creator, but it was now also becoming the lie which promoted the idea that mankind was on the verge of taking a "quantum leap of consciousness."

Just as Sharon had explained so energetically in our long-ago pub conversation, evolution was supposed to be taking man onward and upward. In one book, I read that "humanity was on the threshold of an evolutionary leap, a leap which could occur in a moment of evolutionary time." The author went on to state that he had come to this conclusion through his study of meditation, yoga and other eastern religious techniques.

Then, I started to search out information about the founding fathers of evolution--the men and their motives. It became apparent to me that an accumulation of indisputable facts had not forced them to believe in evolution. Their motives were far less noble. They had been looking for a way to explain away God.

With interest, I read about Erasmus Darwin, the grandfather of Charles Darwin. In the late 1700's, seeds of discontent within the British intellectual community were beginning to take root. One group of heretical thinkers formed an organization called the Lunar Society of Birmingham, which met once a month at the time of the full moon.

This aristocratic group of men sought social change and the advancement of a secular society. Active from 1764 to 1800, the group never included more than fourteen members. These members were, however, some of the most influential men in England, and their primary intention was the removal of the church from a position of power in Great Britain.

The Lunar Society recognized the Bible as the greatest single obstacle to the achievement of its socialist aims. The society concluded that generating disbelief in the Bible would be the most effective way of changing public opinion. Casting doubt on such doctrines as the virgin birth of Jesus Christ or the resurrection would have been too shocking to the culture of that day. Instead, the Lunar Society chose to discredit the biblical accounts of the creation and the flood.

As founder of the Lunar Society, Erasmus Darwin's contribution to the emerging view of evolution was a two-volume work written in 1794-96 called the Zoonomia. Although Charles Darwin was born seven years after his grandfather died, the ideas of Erasmus Darwin deeply influenced his life. Zoonomia expressed the essence of the theory that his grandson announced to the world some five decades later.

Unearthing the roots of evolutionary philosophy opened a whole new realm of understanding for me. A light instantly came on. I could see the effect evolution was going to have on civilization in the future. Chapter one of Paul's epistle to the Romans clearly revealed to me a pattern. When man refuses to place his trust in God and, rather, places it in man, the unavoidable result is a corrupted spiritual dimension. From God, to man, to the "gods", became a central theme in my thinking and my presentations.

During the summer of 1986, Richard Hughes arranged for Larry and me to go to Oklahoma City to meet with a film producer. Pat Matrisciana was attending a Christian conference there. We were sitting at a table during a banquet, when a tall, silver-haired man sat next to me.

"Hi! I just want to give you a copy of, *Gods of the New Age,* a book my wife has written", he grinned. As he handed it to me I saw the name of the author, Caryl Matrisciana.

"So you're Pat Matrisciana?" I asked him.

"Yes, I'm Caryl's husband," he replied.

"Well, you're the guy I came here to meet!" I exclaimed. "Richard Hughes is flying in later today to set up a meeting between us. I'm Roger Oakland."

"I'm here to meet you, too!" he beamed.

After the banquet, I took the book to my room and began

to read it. I read it until my eyes wouldn't stay open. Caryl was describing in her testimony how she had lost her faith in the Biblical God, and became a westernized Hindu. Her story was the counterpart to my own pathway in life. It was as if our lives had supernaturally been directed together.

The following day, as I met with Pat and Richard, I ardently told them about how evolution and Eastern religions were interconnected. I explained how Satan had used evolution to deceive the world. "The whole idea of evolution is the greatest delusion in history," I explained. "Satan has used evolution to blind the minds of our generation. It's a conspiracy authored by Satan."

"That's it!" shouted Pat, springing out his chair. "That's the title for this film. We'll call it "The Evolution Conspiracy!"

For the next few months, Caryl Matrisciana and I corresponded. We agreed that we would co-author a book to go along with the film. For that purpose, God had placed the two of us together as a team. Another aspect of His plan for my ministry had unfolded.

Then came a Sunday evening service at the Eston Full Gospel Church in June of 1987. My pastor, Gil Killam, looked out over the congregation, then spoke with a voice of authority. "I believe God is calling individuals tonight to become involved in full-time missionary work!"

His voice penetrated my heart. I knew that God was using my pastor's voice to speak to me. I'd just turned forty and I had recently prayed, "God, please make me willing to do what you want me to do for the rest of my life. I want to follow you."

As I closed my eyes, in my mind I saw Myrna, myself and our three children, Wade, Bryce, and Angela, standing with me at the altar at the front of our church. We were being prayed for as we were about to leave for California where I was going to become involved in full-time ministry. For a moment, I tried to put this impression out of my mind. It would be absurd for that kind of event to occur. We'd have to leave our family, friends and the farm. It wasn't logical, or even feasible.

Over the past nine years, I'd been involved in ministry for eight months of the year, and had supported myself with income from the family farm. Farming in the late seventies and early eighties had been quite profitable. But things had changed. Now, because of a number of circumstances beyond our control, the farming economy in Saskatchewan was suffering.

For some months now, I'd felt that God was speaking clearly to me about becoming involved in a full-time ministry that would be based in southern California. Although I didn't know how this would occur, I worked on the process of obtaining my U.S. citizenship papers from the U.S. Consulate in Calgary. My father had been an American citizen, and this simplified a normally complex procedure.

In April of 1988, I was in California working on *The Evolution Conspiracy* film. During this time, I met with several different friends and organizations. As usual, I drove to Costa Mesa to visit a man whom God had used in a very strategic way to bless my life and ministry.

Our team had first been invited to hold a seminar at Calvary Chapel, Costa Mesa in June, 1981. Earlier that year, Pastor Chuck Smith had been a speaker at a conference in Regina, Saskatchewan. Someone had given him a set of audio tapes from our "Bible and Science" seminar. He had listened to them on the way back to California and then invited our team to his church to speak. For four evenings, the auditorium was packed with over 3,000 people.

The response to the information was the most encouraging we had received anywhere we had travelled. Calvary Chapel had also supported the production of our first video series and so I was very appreciative of what Chuck Smith and the church had done to expand the ministry.

So, while in Southern California in 1988, I stopped by the church to see if Pastor Chuck was available to see me. As I walked through the door of the Calvary Chapel church office, Chuck was coming out of his private office.

"Roger! How are you? Why don't you come in and bring me up to date on what you've been doing?" I was delighted with the opportunity to share with him my recent discovery regarding the connection of evolution and the New Age philosophy.

"I've just come from the University of San Diego bookstore," I began. Looking down at my bulging briefcase, I said, "You can't believe where evolutionary thinking is headed."

I reached into my briefcase and pulled out a copy of a book called *Kundalini for the New Age*. It had the following subtitle, "A world-renowned Yoga reveals the remarkable source of psychic energy that lies within us all." Handing it to him, and reading from the back cover, I remarked, "See, the author of this book claims that evolution is slowly drawing the human race to a golden future of harmony, peace and happiness, and that 'higher consciousness' will be the natural endowment of every man and woman in the future."

I went on to share with him more about my research on the connection between evolution and the New Age idea, that man was on his way to the evolutionary pathway to higher consciousness. Pastor Chuck was clearly shocked by what I had to say. "We need someone like you to come and deal with these issues here," he commented. "Would you consider coming and joining us here at Calvary Chapel?"

I caught my breath. I told him how I had felt God preparing my family for a move to California.

He smiled and, leaning back in his chair, said, "Well, there's a place for you here if you'd ever like to come." He pointed out the need for producing books, publications, audio and video tapes that would intelligently present a Christian world view. He was talking about the very things I knew God had called me to do.

The previous summer, at a family Bible camp in Northern Alberta, God had clearly spoken to me about the necessity of producing books, audio and visual materials that would distribute the creation-evolution, New Age message on a wide scale. But doing such a thing was simply not possible in a small, Canadian prairie town. I knew that it would involve linking together with others who shared a similar vision and burden. Chuck's words amounted to a confirmation. I heard them loud and clear.

And so, in August 1988, that "glimpse" of my family standing at the altar became a reality. As we drove the 1800 miles from Eston to Los Angeles, I had a lot of time to ponder what was happening. We were leaving a town of 1,400 to become part of the massive Los Angeles metropolitan area of 14 million. The question went through my mind: What did the future hold?

The first year at Calvary Chapel was a difficult one. My expectations of what I believed I would be doing and what I actually ended up doing did not coincide. My previous involvement in ministry was as an itinerant lecturer/speaker. But when I came to Calvary Chapel, it appeared as if I were being molded into an assistant pastor's role.

I questioned whether or not Myrna and I had made the right move. Weighing all of the factors together, on April 27, 1989, I packed my pickup truck with all my books and research and headed back to the farm for seeding. I felt as if I had totally missed God's call. Discouraged and broken-hearted that things had not materialized the way we expected, I wondered if my involvement in ministry was a mistake. I felt like I had failed God. My vision was dead.

One cold morning, during seeding time, when I was working on a piece of farm equipment, I heard God speak clearly to my understanding again. It was another of these times in my life when I knew that I'd had a divine appointment. I began to think of the millions of people around the world who had never heard about Jesus Christ. My heart ached as I thought of the consequences.

And then, in a still, silent impression, the thought came. "Are you ready to go back to California and follow Me? I have a plan for your life, a plan that is not finished."

Later that day, Myrna called me from our California home. She informed me that she was convinced I had made the wrong decision in leaving. "I think we should try it for one more year," she said. "I don't think that God is through with us here yet."

I agreed and related to her what had already happened to me previously that day.

In a few weeks' time, I returned to California. I was able to sit down with Pastor Chuck in his office. He gave me the opportunity to express my frustrations about my first year at Calvary Chapel. Recognizing that my calling was in outreach and missionary work, he said he would introduce me to other Calvary Chapel pastors at two upcoming conferences, one in the state of New York and the other in Palm Springs (there are approximately 400 churches around the world affiliated with the mother church - Calvary Chapel of Costa Mesa, California). From that moment on, my ministry became an outreach of Calvary Chapel of Costa Mesa.

Doors of opportunity to hold seminars on creation-evolution and exposing the New Age were now open throughout the United States, as well as in many parts of the world. Furthermore, I began to establish relationships with well-known ministries, such as the Institute For Creation Research, the Christian Research Institute, the Far East Broadcasting Company and Hal Lindsey Ministries, all based in southern California.

The ministry to the uttermost parts of the earth had begun. The call to **"Go Tell It on the Mountain"** was finally becoming a reality.

Chapter Thirteen

TYRANNOSAURUS REX

W here had the time gone? More than twenty years had slipped by since I'd first driven down this same street to the university grounds, my own father at the wheel of his car. Now I was the father, and I was driving my two sons toward the same destination. It all seemed unreal.

Time had certainly flown by. Wade, my oldest son, and Bryce, who was one year younger, were now both teenagers. This was the first time I had been able to take them to the University of Saskatchewan where I'd spent almost ten years of my life. I had talked to them a number of times about the "good old days" there, during the late sixties and the early seventies. Now here we were, about to explore the campus that had been so much a part of my life.

I located a parking place, and we headed out on foot to explore the campus. It didn't take me long to see that many changes had taken place. Not only had the parking fees and student body doubled, but the number of buildings had also increased. Large, empty areas that had once been filled with trees and grass when I had last been on campus had been replaced by impressive new structures.

Paved sidewalks that had teemed with students walking hurriedly from one building to another were almost empty. During the summer months most of the students were away from campus, working at various jobs. We had chosen a good day to browse around and look at some of the buildings and classrooms where I had both attended classes and taught.

"Let's start our tour by getting a good view of the campus from the Arts Tower," I suggested to the boys. The Arts and Science Building was situated on the western side of a large open area known as the Bowl. The Bowl, laid out in an oval shape, was surrounded by buildings on all sides. The University buildings were well-known for their picturesque appearance. Each had been surfaced by stone masons in greystone, limestone, and Tyndall stone (pre-cut slabs quarried in Tyndall, Manitoba), giving the campus a unique look that few other Canadian universities could match.

We walked into the Arts building, stepped into the elevator and pushed the button for the eleventh floor, the uppermost point on campus. As we were heading towards the top floor, I couldn't help but remember the hundreds of times I had pushed that same button in the past. The Philosophy Department held the majority of its classes on the eleventh floor.

Leaving the elevator, we started down the hall until we found a room with windows facing west. Looking out, we could see the large University Hospital complex situated on the banks of South Saskatchewan River.

"Is that where Mom used to work as a nurse?"

"Yes, that's right. I can even point out to you the exact location where she worked." The southerly wing of the fourth floor was the obstetrics department where she had been based for a number of years during the early seventies. "In fact," I quickly recalled, "that's not only where your mother worked. It's also the place where you were born!"In order to get to the Biology Building, we had to work our way down the hall to the front door of the Arts Building and then walk half way around the Bowl. Posters were hung on both sides of the hall announcing several events that were taking place at different times throughout the summer-school schedule. I was glad to see that one of them advertised an evening debate on the ever-controversial subject of Creation vs. Evolution.

A large, open room appeared directly in front of us. Over to our right side, we saw an immense dinosaur skeleton standing in an upright position, glaring down upon us as if it were ready to attack. The area, which appeared to a be a museum in the process of construction, was buzzing with activity. The great dinosaur was surrounded by scaffolding, and three workmen were struggling to lift its large head into position.

Above the dinosaur I could see a second floor area which overlooked the museum. A number of people were gathered there, watching the crew at work. From our position, it appeared that someone was getting ready to give a speech. We made our way to where a janitor was sweeping the floor, hoping to find out what was going on.

"What's all this commotion about?" I asked. The man looked at me as if I were the only person on the campus grounds who wasn't aware of the significance of this great event. "This is the special dedication of Tyrannosaurus," he beamed. "Every staff member in this building has been awaiting this occasion for a very long time. You must be a visitor around here."

Yes I am," I replied. "But today is a lot like being back home. I spent ten years of my life in that building right over there," I said, pointing to the exterior surface of the old biology complex. "I thought I would bring my sons around and have a look at the old place again."

"How many years ago was that?" asked the man, leaning on his broom. I had to stop for a minute and think. "1975 was the year I left here. Let's see. That's more than a decade ago. Man, I can't believe so much time has gone by!"

"Well, you'll find there have been a lot of changes since then. Why don't you go upstairs to the second floor where all the excitement is going on? If you were around here for that many years, you're sure to meet up with somebody you know."

We took his advice and headed up the stairs, making our way closer to the group that we had seen overlooking the balcony. About thirty people were huddled around a man who was holding a silver tray. He appeared to be preparing to make a speech. Beside him was a table with two bottles of champagne, plus a number of glasses. Everyone's attention was directed toward the dinosaur as a few final adjustments were being made. Suddenly, there was a tremendous cheer, and the man holding the silver tray began to speak.

"I am sure you are aware," he thundered, with a thick, German accent, "that this day marks a great milestone in the history of the Biology and Geology departments of the University of Saskatchewan. We have all waited for the completion of the great "Tyrannosaurus rex," which has come to us from the American Museum of Natural History in New York. What a splendid job these workmen have done in assembling this great creature! And they have done it all in record time." There was more cheering and clapping as the three men on the scaffold took a bow.

The speech continued. "I'm sure all of you are aware of the controversy that exists over the proper stance of this magnificent four-legged creature," he said, his deep, sonorous voice echoing through the building. "Some people believe that Tyrannosaurus should be assembled in a crouched position, touching the ground with all four legs. It has been our choice to erect Tyrannosaurus in an upright stature. However, whether he stands straight up, or lies down, is of no significance at all. The major point is that the mighty Tyrannosaurus rex, king of the Cretaceous era of the past, stands here in this museum as a monument to the 'evolution' of life."

Another thunderous round of applause echoed throughout the building. The gentleman making the speech cleared his throat and started again. "As all of you know, the purpose of this museum is to follow the evolutionary thread of life through the millions of years of geological time. It is our objective and desire that every person who walks through the doors of this museum will be awe-struck by the overwhelming evidence that you and I are here because of our evolutionary past."

The champagne bottles were cracked open and the cheering resumed. While the speech had been going on, I'd let my eyes sweep across the crowd. Every face reflected satisfaction and agreement with all that had been said. Somehow, the faces that I was observing all looked strangely familiar. Who were these people? Where had I seen them before?

Wade jabbed me in the side. "What are you staring at, Dad?" he interrupted. Suddenly, I realized who these people were. They were my old colleagues--men and women I had worked with when I was a member of this department. They were still here. All was the same, except everyone looked older. An overwhelming feeling of sadness crept over me.

The boys were ready to go so we headed out of the area. My mind was buzzing with activity. These were men and women that I had once known! Should I go over and interrupt their celebration and tell them what had happened to me?

We made our exit through doors which opened into the second-floor lounge. The same Coke machine was standing in the same corner. We started down the hall. The same rooms with the same numbers above the doors were still there. The same smell of formaldehyde permeated the air. A few more steps and we were in front of my old office.

It seemed so strange to me. It was as if the people that I had left behind were locked in a timeless dimension. The university was a cocoon, a kind of never-never land where everybody, even the faculty, could be like Peter Pan and never grow up.

Although the sun was shining, darkness seemed to overshadow the campus as I looked around. The University of Saskatchewan was only one small bastion of evolutionary thinking. All over North America and the western world hundreds of millions of people had been deluded by the greatest hoax in the history of mankind: Darwinian evolution - mankind's attempt to explain away God.

I was soon to discover that an alternative scenario was

being acted out across the sea. Behind the Iron Curtain, where God had been banished and the "religion" of Marxism violently enforced, there was a totally different point of view. There, alive and growing in the spiritual darkness, were countless men and women, yearning to hear of a Creator God. They knew, all too well, that life without Him was empty, meaningless and without hope.

Chapter Fourteen

GOOD MORNING, RUSSIA

"**F**ive more minutes, Mr. Oakland, and you'll be on!" It was just a few days before Christmas, 1991, and I was about to appear on "Good Morning Russia," with a potential viewing audience of over 200 million.

That great nation was still reeling from the news: it was the morning after Mikhail Gorbachev had announced the final countdown to the collapse of the Soviet Union. "The Bear" that had terrified the world for so long, that trillions of American dollars worth of nuclear armaments had failed to wound, was now about die, unceremoniously, with barely a whimper.

I was staring at the monitor at the Soviet State Television

studio in downtown Moscow. A military man was being interviewed. He represented the Marxist Soviet system which, as far as I was concerned had centered around the worship of man.

"He's a Russian general," explained Fred Lutsenko, my translator and the Canadian director of ORA (Orphans Refugee Aid) International, a German-based humanitarian organization.

"What's he saying?" I asked, intrigued with what was going on, well aware that I was watching history unfold before me.

Fred turned to me and responded, "He's being asked to tell the people that there's nothing to fear, that everything's under control. He's putting down people's concern over who has control of the 'nuclear button.'"

I was incredulous. Here I was, light years away from my farm in Canada, watching the atheistic-based superpower that had dominated over seventy years of world affairs being declared financially and spiritually bankrupt. History was in the making, right before my eyes.

My own countdown with destiny was fast approaching. Within a few short minutes, I would be sitting in the general's seat, also being interviewed. I would not be discussing military, political, or economic problems in the Soviet Empire. My subject was the most important question on earth, "Is there a God?"

I nervously walked over to the window and surveyed the skyline of the great city of Moscow, stretching out in all directions as far as the eye could see. Nagging questions rose up inside me: Can I handle this responsibility? Am I qualified to do this? What on earth am I going to say?

For more than seven terrible decades the leadership of the

Soviet Union had been fighting something they claimed didn't exist--God. The utopia Marx and Lenin had promised never had materialized. Instead, the people had been held in bondage by fear. The Russian Revolution had cursed millions of men, women and children with a system that robbed them materially while impoverishing their spirits with deceit and corruption.

Standing beside me was Dr. Dmitri Kouznetsov, the pioneer of the creationist movement in the former Soviet Union. This 36-year-old, casually dressed Russian scientist, with three doctorate degrees, had arranged this extraordinary interview.

A book I had co-authored, *The Evidence for Creation,* had been released the day before. The first book on the subject of creation ever to be published within the former Soviet Union, sixty thousand copies had just rolled off the press.

As I waited to address the biggest audience of my life, I began to recall the events that had taken place over the past fourteen years. I smiled and said quietly under my breath, "This is a long way from Avon Lee, where I held my first-ever seminar on creationism."

On the way back from that gathering, my mentor, Pastor McLean, had shared some verses with me from the book of Joshua 1:5-6 which had comforted him through many a difficult time. I ruffled through the pages of my Bible and came to the place where I had underlined the encouraging words:

"There shall not be any man
Able to stand before thee all the days of thy life.
As I was with Moses, so I will be with thee.
I shall not fail thee nor forsake thee.
Be strong and of good courage."

Pastor McLean had told me, "God has promised to always give you the words to say at the right moment." At that moment I assured myself that, however nervous I might be, the Lord really would be with me. My thoughts were interrupted when the studio manager pushed open the door and barked something out in Russian. Fred interpreted for me. "It's time to go to the studio," he said. This was it! I uttered one more silent prayer for strength, tightly clasped my Bible, and headed onto the "Good Morning Russia" set.

I shook hands with the host, Michael Solntsevn, who spoke some English. "I'll ask the questions in English and then your friend here," he said, pointing to Fred, "can translate for us. But first, we have a one-minute excerpt of you speaking here in Moscow during the past few days."

The Russian anchorman asked for quiet on the set, and a woman began narrating from a prepared script. I watched the monitor and saw myself speaking at the National Academy of Sciences, addressing some of Russia's top scientists and philosophers. It hardly seemed possible that this had taken place, but now it was actually being beamed into millions of homes across the vast nation.

As the monitor went black, the Russian interviewer, in his mid-thirties, turned to me and asked in a voice that was resonant, yet soft and friendly, "As you are no doubt aware, our country is in the process of collapse. People are wanting answers. For years we were told that there is no God. What can you tell our people? Is there a God?"

As he ended his question, I felt a sudden surge of energy fill my body. I leaned forward on the edge of my seat. "Being here on this program is a testimony that God does exist," I began firmly. "For many years of my life, I believed in evolution. I was convinced that it could explain the existence of life, but several years ago I became a creationist, then a Christian. The reason I am here, speaking in Russia, is to proclaim that there is a Creator and there is evidence for creation."

"What is this evidence for creation?" asked Michael, locking his eyes on mine. I handed him a copy of my book and he leafed through it and held up the pages to the camera.

"The observable evidence comes from biology, geology and archaeology, all of which support the creation position," I said. "The world of God and the Word of God agree!"

"What has been the response here to your teachings?"

"It's been extremely positive," I replied. "Many people have told me that they had always equated Darwinian evolution with Marxist teaching. Now, having seen the failure of Marxism, they are open to hearing about a biblical world view. One of my meetings was with the Moscow Creation Fellowship, founded by Dr. Kouznetsov, who is one of your nation's top scientists. There are now more than 140 members of this organization, which was founded in May of 1990."

The young Russian T.V. personality listened intently to what I was saying. "Has anyone opposed what you have said while you have been here?" he asked.

"Yes, there have been a few," I replied truthfully, "but only a few. Overall, I am overwhelmed by the positive response I've received here."

The host then said, "Unfortunately, our interview this morning only allows us a brief few minutes. What message would you like to leave with our audience?"

I took a deep breath, then launched into my final words.

"For the past seventy years," I said, "you have been ₁orced to place your trust in man, and the consequences have left this great nation in a state of chaos. This morning, I believe that God wants all of you watching this program to place your trust in Him. He wants everyone to have a relationship with Him. He is the Creator. There is evidence that He created everything. Turn to Him, not to man."

As the interview concluded, and Michael went onto another pre-taped part of the show, he handed me his card and said enthusiastically, "Anytime you are in Moscow, Roger, you can be a guest on this program."

As we left the studio, I pulled my overcoat tightly around my shoulders. Dr. Kouznetsov, who is normally stoic and expressionless, hugged me emotionally and spoke with passion. "The information God has given you to share with my people is very important so they can come to Christ! God has brought you and me together. How I thank Him that He's allowed this great miracle to happen!"

Tears began to flood my eyes. "Dima," I said, "I can't believe it! This is incredible. How could this possibly have happened?" For the moment, I was searching for natural explanations.

He quietly replied, "Roger, with God, all things are possible."

It was an exultant team that climbed into Dr. Kouznetsov's car outside the headquarters of Soviet State Television on Friday, December 13, 1991. What an odd team we were: a farmer from Saskatchewan, and a renowned scientist from Moscow. By God's grace we had become partners, helping to pioneer the creationist movement in what had once been the cradle of communism. Only the Creator of the universe could have bonded two very different individuals together with such love and appreciation for each other. We headed out onto the Moscow streets, past the drably dressed men and women who waited in block-long lines outside shops; The scenery was drab, and the people's mood was grim. Nonetheless, I wanted to shout with joy.

I had met Dr. Kouznetsov in a most unlikely way. I had received a telephone call at my office, in February, 1990, from Dr. John Morris of the Institute For Creation Research in San Diego, California. During that conversation, he had suggested that I attend a lecture by a Russian scientist on the subject of creation. The opportunity to hear a Russian creationist fascinated me.

So I headed to Newhall, California, and attended an afternoon lecture in a church with only eighty people in attendance. When the man walked in to give his presentation, all eyes, including my own, were on him. I was surprised to see how young he was, considering the credentials he carried.

But what was even more amazing to me was his testimony. He didn't speak about scientific things. Instead, he offered the simple, powerful story of how he had become a Christian. He explained that he had first become a creationist, and then a Christian. My heart leapt with excitement as I heard his words. His was exactly the same path I had taken myself.

At the conclusion of the meeting, I had to rush to another appointment, so I wasn't able to talk to him personally. However, I left some material with Dr. George Howe, from Master's College in the San Fernando Valley, who was the coordinator of the meeting. I asked him to pass it on to the Russian scientist, left my card, some of my audio tapes and books, and went on my way.

A week later, the phone rang at my house. It was Dr. Kouznetsov, calling from the East Coast of the United States.

"You must come to Russia," he shouted into the phone. "Your information is very important for my people to hear!" He explained that Dr. Duane Gish, Vice President of the Institute For Creation Research, would be traveling to Moscow in May of 1990 as his special guest.

"Would it be possible for you to come along too?" he asked.

Knowing that I didn't have the funds to cover the cost of such a trip, I asked him if he would give me some time to try and raise the necessary support. The following day, I submitted a request to the board of Calvary Chapel of Costa Mesa. Almost instantaneously, I received the finances to make the trip.

So on May 10, 1990, I found myself on a Pan Am 747 jumbo jet, flying from New York to Moscow. The trip was historic. Dr. Gish was to be the first American in history to be officially invited to make a specific presentation on creation in Russia. At that time, perestroika was allowing freedom of thought, but communism still had a strong foothold.

Those ten days were unlike any I had lived before. The people's hunger for the creation message was beyond my comprehension. It was "harvest time" in the Soviet Union, and the workers were few. I could see how the message that God had laid upon my heart was vital, now that the lid of communism had been lifted. I thought a lot about how I could become one of the workers in this great harvest field.

The following September, Dr. Kouznetsov returned to the United States and stayed at my home for several days. During that time, I was able to introduce him to Hal Lindsey, Chuck Smith and Hank Hanegraaff. Through radio and television, my Russian friend had a national platform to communicate his vision--he wanted to reach his own people with the creation message as the basis of the Gospel.

"Your book on creation must be translated into the Russian language for my people to read," he told me one day as we drove along one of Los Angeles' never-ending freeways. "You see, Roger, I have a problem. I find it difficult to communicate with the average person in Russia because my lectures are too technical. Your information would be easy for them to understand. It would clearly let them know that there is a God!"

About a month after he had left, I submitted a second request to the board of Calvary Chapel, this time asking if they would assist in the translation and publishing of, *The Evidence For Creation.* Once again, they kindly provided the necessary financial assistance.

In March of 1991, another event occurred, wonderfully confirming that God's sovereign hand was upon this process. I was in Kelowna, British Columbia, speaking at a city-wide conference with Hank Hanegraaff, president of the Christian Research Institute in Irvine, California. He is the well-known host of the nationally broadcast "Bible Answer Man" radio program.

A breakfast was being held for thirty local pastors. Seated at my table of eight were a couple of men who spoke to each other in Russian. In order to make conversation, I told one of them, who also spoke English, that I had been to Moscow the previous year. He conveyed this to his partner, Vladimir, who was from Riga, Latvia.

"What were you doing in Moscow?" he asked through his interpreter.

"I was there, along with Dr. Gish, to present creationism to Russian scientists," I explained.

The Latvian's face lit up as he blurted out, "I think I may know the scientist who coordinated those meetings. It was Dr. Kouznetsov, wasn't it?"

"You know Dr. Kouznetsov?" I asked incredulously.

The odds against this happening were staggering. In the Soviet Union there are more than 280 million people and in North America, over 250 million. Here we were, seated at the same table and sharing a common friend.

I then told him about my book, *The Evidence for Creation,* which had been translated into Russian in Moscow. An unusual expression covered his face. "I saw your book in Moscow before I came to Canada," he said. "My brother-in-law, Alexander Semchenko, is the head of the company that is publishing your book." These "coincidences" were staggering. Clearly our meeting had been arranged by God's sovereign appointment.

Vladimir went on to say that he had been approached by the Latvian Department of Education, asking his help in putting together a curriculum on biblical creationism for the local schools. On his way to Canada, he had stopped in Moscow to see if any material on creation was available in the Russian language. There he'd seen my book at a christian publisher. Later that day, my new Latvian friend invited me to visit his homeland.

The earliest possible time that I could go to Latvia was December 1991, which was when my book was due to be released in Moscow. It made perfect sense for me to coordinate the Latvian trip with the Moscow trip. Meetings were arranged for me in both places by Fred Lutsenko of ORA Canada and Dr. Kouznetsov.

That second trip to the Soviet Union, in December of 1991, increased my understanding immensely. I could now see the tragic consequences of Darwinian evolutionary brainwashing, so forcefully propagated through the indoctrination of Marxist atheism. Not only had millions of people been duped by the "evolution delusion", but they had also been left physically, spiritually and morally bankrupt. The land was in chaos.

The people's openness to hear an alternative to the Darwin-Marxist philosophy had continued to grow since my 1990 trip. The "evolution delusion" had removed the concept of creation from an entire society. Now it appeared that many individuals were fully prepared to fill the void within themselves with another delusion - the idea that man can become God.

Throughout those two weeks, I observed that the interest in the occult, the supernatural, Eastern religions, and New Age teachings had continued to expand. Every facet of the culture had been influenced. In Riga, for instance, during a tour of a medical facility, I noticed one whole floor of a medical building being utilized for shamanistic healing techniques. These included the use of pentagrams, pyramids, crystals, and Yoga therapy.

One night in Moscow, I was watching the late news. At the end of the newscast I was startled to see astrological signs appear on the screen.

"What's going on?" I asked Fred.

"It's the evening astrology report. They broadcast it here every day there's such a strong interest in it. "

But the most amazing indication that the New Age had come of age in the former Soviet Union was evidenced when I spoke on the subject: "Evolution: The Basis of New Age Philosophy" at the National Academy of Sciences in Moscow. The meeting consisted of some of Russia's top scientists and philosophers.

During a one-hour presentation, I asserted that evolution, Eastern religion, and New Age were ideas that were interconnected. After the lecture, I was challenged in a two-hour question and answer period by several of the participants. It became apparent that many of them were willing to reject Darwinian evolution because of the lack of evidence, but now had embraced metaphysical ideas in an attempt to explain the origins and history of life. Three of the scientists who claimed they were atheists indicated by their own statements that they actually were pantheists - they believed that everything was God.

The chairman of the discussion concluded the meeting with a shocking statement: "Your comments condemning Eastern religions have troubled me," he said. "I have just finished writing a new book called, *The New Man for the New Era*. I believe that out of the chaos that surrounds us now, a new man will emerge--a man that will become ecologically responsible." He went on to say that he believed man should have a special, worshipful relationship with nature.

The chairman concluded "In the future, we will see a political and religious union that will enhance this relationship between man and nature and thus there will be utopia on planet earth."

I wondered if my translator were getting this right. I couldn't believe what I was hearing. His statement was certainly prophetic from a biblical perspective.

This was the very thing that God had called me to warn people about. I was to point them toward the Creator and away from the worship of the creation.

I took a deep breath and began to speak.

"You speak of a new man for the new era, and a political and religious system that will bring utopia in the future," I began. "What you are predicting is exactly what the Bible describes as the consequence of rejecting the evidence for God's existence.

"The words of the apostle Paul recorded in the Bible in Romans 1 state that rejecting the overwhelming evidence for creation leads man to worship the creation rather than the Creator. The Bible further clarifies that one day there will be a religious and political system that will unite the world together, but not to bring about utopia, as you believe, but rather judgment and destruction.

"You speak about a new man for the new era. That's what Karl Marx promised. Just look out on your streets to see the consequences of that thinking. Placing trust in man has left this nation totally bankrupt. The Bible also talks about a new man but only in terms of a 'new creation in Christ Jesus.'"

I pointed to the directors of ORA International, seated to my right, Heinz Floreck, the founder, and Fred Lutsenko, the Canadian director.

"This organization, which has sponsored my trip is also here to distribute food, clothing and medical supplies to suffering children and old people in Moscow," I said. "These men are Christians, and are here to help your people because of their relationship with the Creator. We are commanded to first love God and then our neighbors as ourselves. That's why these men are here helping you.

"Maybe I have offended you by pointing out what I know to be the serious consequences of believing in Eastern metaphysical thought. But I can't apologize. Turning away from God and turning to the practices of the occult will destroy your nation more catastrophically than ever."

I concluded with words from the Prophet Jeremiah 11:9. "Again the Lord said to me, 'there is a conspiracy among the men of Judah and the inhabitants of Jerusalem.'" The scripture went on to say that God's people had turned away from Him and were joining in the worship of the pagans. The prophet was warning them that judgment was ahead.

"Evolution has removed God from your thinking," I continued. "You men and women are scientists and philosophers so I am going to challenge you to perform an experiment. Turn to the God of the Bible. If you do, I promise that your lives will be totally changed."

At the end of the meeting there was a buzz of activity in the room as people paired off to talk in an animated fashion. No one spoke to me. I felt defeated, especially since the chairman had been so powerful in his closing remarks.

As I was picking up my notes and putting them in my briefcase, I was approached by a grey-haired man in his late fifties, wearing a pin-striped suit. He was very excited about something. At first, I couldn't tell whether he was for me or against me.

He smiled, and said through a translator, "The information you've presented today is revolutionary. It's what our country needs to hear. I am the editor of *The Journal of Science and Religion*. During the 1950's, our magazine was founded by the Communists, to spread propaganda and lies about Christians. But since perestroika, it has been devoted to expressing the view of all religions. Eighty percent of the articles in our publication are devoted to the very things that you have exposed today."

"We have very little written from a Christian point of view. I would like to see a balance. Would you be willing to write articles for my magazine, telling people about the telling people about the Creator?"

I told him that I wanted to talk to him some more and agreed that he could interview me in my hotel room a couple of days later. I also gave him permission to freely quote from my books and other articles and promised to submit some material to him for future publication.

Part way through the interview, the man stopped and, with tears in his eyes, said, "Roger, I want you to pray with me. I'd like to have the same faith in God that you have."

For a moment, I didn't know what to say. Then an idea came to mind. I reached into my briefcase and gave him the only copy I had left of, *The Evidence For Creation.*

He looked at the cover of the book and his eyes glowed with appreciation.

"Now", I said, "what I have just done is an illustration. It's meant to give you a very small glimpse of what God has done for you. I just gave you the only English version of *The Evidence For Creation* that I have here in Russia.

"But God gave 'His only begotten Son, that whosoever believeth in Him should not perish but have everlasting life.'

"All you need to do is accept God's gift and receive it. A gift is not a gift until you take it. You took my book, and by doing so, the giving process was completed. Now it's your choice whether or not you take the gift of God's Son."

With that, we prayed together, and the man gladly received Jesus Christ as his Savior. The radiance of the gospel had come into his life. He pointed to the front cover of *The Evidence For Creation* book which showed a shaft of light coming from outer space and touching the world.

"This book's cover graphically illustrates light shining upon the earth. I believe that the message contained within it can bring light to my dark country."

I smiled. "Yes. That's my prayer, not only for this country but for people around the world."

How humbled I felt. God's grace had allowed me to bring light to a land that had been locked in spiritual gloom for seven decades. In fact, God had done what He'd promised to do. He'd saved me from my own darkness, and then sent me out as a bearer of His illuminating message.

Tears of joy flooded my eyes. "May God send the light!" I said to the man. "Let there be Light!"

EPILOGUE

Now that you have read through *Let There Be Light* in its entirety, I hope one thing has become exceptionally clear to you: the miracle-working power of the grace of God. The statement of the apostle Paul recorded in I Corinthians 1:26-30 describes my personal feelings better than any words I could put together on my own:

"For consider your calling, brethren, that there were not many wise according to the flesh, not many mighty, not many noble; but God has chosen the foolish things of the world to shame the wise, and God has chosen the weak things of the world to shame the things that are strong, and the base things of the world and the despised, God has chosen; the things that are not, that He might nullify the things that are, that no man should be able to boast before God. But by His doing you are in Christ Jesus."

The spiritual journey of my life, from childhood into adult maturity, has not been a unique one. In my travels throughout the world over the past several years, I have talked with many other men and women who have traveled along the same trail. They believed in God when they were children, lost faith while studying at the shrine of humanism, and then experienced a spiritual awakening which introduced them to the miraculous grace of God. For many of us who followed that particular path, the recognition that God's Word and God's world agree has played a key role in our conversion from darkness to light.

The dynamic revelation that the Creator existed was the first step to my transformation. Recognizing God's holiness and perfection in light of my own sinful nature and imperfection was the second. It was only then that I first fully understood my need for a Redeemer--Jesus Christ.

The title we chose for this book, *Let There Be Light*, is intended to have a three-fold meaning.

First of all, it reflects one of the basic principles of the Genesis account of origins.

Secondly, it refers to the saving power of God's Holy Spirit to radically transform lives from darkness to light.

And thirdly, it projects the desire of my heart that the message of creation evangelism be spread over the entire earth. What more essential message of hope could there be for our troubled planet during these last, strategic days of time?

PROJECT: LET THERE BE LIGHT

I was first invited to Moscow in May, 1990 by Dr. Dmitri Kouznetsov to speak to Russian scientists and educators about the topic of Biblical creation. Then came the initial publication of the book, *The Evidence for Creation,* in December, 1991.

Since those two events, doors have miraculously swung open throughout the former Soviet Union. Lectures and conferences presented to scientists, educators and students in Russia and other former Soviet Republics have been received with an overwhelming, enthusiastic response--above what we could ask or think.

In December of 1992, our path was directed to the office of Dr. Alexander Asmolov, Deputy Minister of Education for Russia. After reviewing the Russian version of *The Evidence For Creation* book, we were asked by the Russian Department of Education if it would be possible for us to provide them with copies of the book for their schools so children could read about the evidence for creation (there are 43 million students in school throughout Russia).

The significance of this opportunity is paramount. For over seventy years the schools throughout Russia were used as virtual seminaries for atheism, which was the basis of the Marxist communist philosophy. The idea of a Creator God, who brought the universe into existence, was scoffed at. Worse yet, any teaching about God was literally legislated out of the nation's culture. But today, all that has changed.

What an amazing opportunity He has placed before us!

By December of 1993 approximately 500,000 copies of the Russian version of *The Evidence for Creation* book will be in print. This is the first stage toward our goal of 2 million books. We are grateful to the Lord for leading Pastor Chuck Smith and the Board of Calvary Chapel of Costa Mesa, California; Pastor Mike MacIntosh of Horizon Christian Fellowship; Pastor Lloyd Pulley of Calvary Chapel, Old Bridge, New Jersey; as well as numerous other churches and individuals, for generously assisting us to fund the first phase of *Project: Let There Be Light.*

Demand for the book and opportunities to distribute it on a massive scale continue to be placed before us. Several radio and TV programs have been broadcast throughout Russia, making people aware of the availability of the book. Meanwhile, CoMission, a cooperative effort by numerous Christian organizations from North America dedicated to reach the former Soviet Union with the gospel, has selected the book as a tool for evangelism. As a result, the book will be distributed to schools, teachers, institutes and universities all over Russia and many other countries where the Russian language is spoken.

It is our prayer that God will speak to the hearts of His people to help bring to fulfillment the completion of this project. The expense of printing and distributing this book in Russia amounts to a small fraction of the cost in North America. For a small investment, a tremendous amount can be accomplished. Will you pray about how you or your church might participate in responding to this God-given opportunity? Let's work together to impact the lives of millions of Russian people for the cause of Christ.

**Donations designated to "Project: Let There Be Light"
may be mailed to:**

Understand the Times
Roger Oakland Ministries
P.O. Box 27239
Santa Ana, CA 92799
U.S.A

OR

Understand The Times
Roger Oakland Ministries
P.O. Box 1160
Eston, Saskatchewan SOL 1AO
Canada

THIS IS A TAX DEDUCTIBLE ORGANIZATION IN
BOTH THE UNITED STATES AND CANADA

About the co-author:

Dan Wooding has authored some twenty-five books and is the founder and international director of ASSIST Ministries based in Garden Grove, California. He is also a syndicated newspaper columnist and a commentator on the UPI Radio Network in Washington, D.C.

Some books by Dan Wooding:

Junkies are People Too
Stresspoint
I Thought Terry Dene Was Dead
Exit The Devil (with Trevor Dearing)
Train of Terror (with Mini Loman)
Rick Wakeman, the Caped Crusader
King Squealer (with Maurice O'Mahoney)
Farewell Leicester Square (with Henry Hollis)
Uganda Holocaust (with Ray Barnett)
Miracles in Sin City (with Howard Cooper)
God's Smuggler to China (with Brother David and Sarah Bruce)
Prophets of Revolution (with Peter Asael Gonzales)
God's Agent (with Brother Andrew)
Guerilla for Christ (with Salu Daka Ndebele)
Million Dollar Promise (with Duane Logsdon)
Twenty-Six Lead Soldiers
Secret Missions
Singing In the Dark (with Barry Taylor)
Lost for Words (with Stuart Mill)
Brother Andrew

AUDIO TAPES OF
SIX PART SEMINAR SERIES

The Evidence For Creation

How and when did life begin? Was it the result
of random chance processes over millions of
years of time, or was life designed by a Creator.

"The Evidence For Creation" audio tape series
examines the fundamental principles of the
evolution and creation models and tests them
against the observable evidence.

Understand The Times

The **Understand The Times** audio tape series
is designed to educate people as to what is
taking place in the world around us from a
biblical perspective. It challenges and equips
the listener to be better prepared for the times
in which we are living.

VIDEOS

These 4 videos are ideal as teaching tools in Christian Schools, Sunday School and Home Bible Studies.

The Evidence For Creation

The subject of origins has been a controversial issue between supporters of the two opposing views — creation and evolution.

This video examines the basic principles of the biblical account and shows how it is supported by the facts of biology and geology.

Evolution: Fact or Fiction

Many scientists today claim the evolutionary world view is the only acceptable explanation for the origin and history of life. Other scientists claim that this is not true.

This video examines the foundational principles of the evolutionary model and examines them in light of the observable evidence.

VIDEOS

Ancient Man: Created or Evolved

The subject of the origin and history of mankind has triggered heated debate between supporters of the two opposing views — creation and evolution.

This video examines both models and tests them against the evidence found in the fossil record and the remains left by ancient civilization.

The Death of the Dinosaur

Dinosuar extinction is a subject that seems to fascinate just about everyone. The fossilized remains of dinosaurs have been found buried in the layers of the earth all over the world. What happened to them? Did they die out gradually, or were they destroyed by a global catastrophe?

"The Death of the Dinosaur" examines the mystery of dinosaur extinction by evaluating the observable evidence and comparing it with two opposite world views — creation or evolution.

VIDEOS

The Evolution Conspiracy

A documentary presenting the creation-evolution debate in an appealing format featuring some of the world's most influential experts on both sides.

BOOKS

The Evidence For Creation

Designed for the layman, this book examines and visually illustrates the creation and evolution models of origins and tests them against the observable evidence.

It is an excellent resource for strengthening the faith of believers, as well as providing valuable information to share with those who have rejected the biblical model of origins.

BOOKS

Understand the Times

This book presents a basic biblical understanding concerning the beliefs, teachings and events sweeping the world today. It is written in an easy to understand format and answers the question: Could we be living in the generation that will witness the return of Jesus Christ for His church? The reader is challenged to awaken to reality by looking to the Bible for solid insight into what is happening in the world, why these things are happening, and where we are headed in the future.

The Evolution Conspiracy

What was once a classroom debate now reaches into every corner of our lives. In this alarming exposé, the author shows that the raging war between evolution and creation is not a battle between <u>science</u> and religion. It's a battle between <u>religion</u> and religion — with social, moral and eternal consequences for us and our children.

For information on how to receive a catalogue of Roger Oakland's materials and/or be placed on the mailing list of Understand the Times: Roger Oakland Ministries,

Write to:

Understand the Times
Roger Oakland Ministries
P.O. Box 27239
Santa Ana
CA 92799

1(800) 689 1888